ARIADNE

The Usborne
Big book
of
Science
things to make
and
do

Rebecca Gilpin and Leonie Pratt

Designed and illustrated by Josephine Thompson

Additional design and illustrations by
Samantha Meredith, Erica Harrison, Katie Lovell,
Jessica Johnson, Katrina Fearn, Helen Edmonds,
Abigail Brown, Antonia Miller

Steps illustrated by Molly Sage

Stickers by Stella Baggott

Photographs by Howard Allman

Edited by Fiona Watt

Consultant: Dr. Andrew West

contents

4   About this book

6   Bubbling wizard's brew

8   Zappy zoomer

10   Fingerprint fun

11   Detective work

12   Sail cars

14   Spooky shadow puppets

16   Mystery meeting map

18   Bobbing bouncing raisins

19   Layered liquids

20   Sparkly space picture

22   Beany bags

24   Floating ball game

25   Head to head

26   Tropical reef painting

28   Dangly monkeys

30   Melted chocolate circles

32   Rocket patterns

33   Folded robot

34   Leaf prints

36   Fishbowl spinner

37   Shark flickbook

38   Swirly snake

40   Mirror magic

42   Lemon slice ice cubes

43   Floating ice boat

44   Flying fish windsock

46   Tea-painted crocodile

48   Fluttering ghost

Stickers

49	Zooming balloon rocket	72	Salty dragon painting
50	Rock and roll eggs	74	Singing bottles
52	Watery whale painting	75	Panpipe straws
54	Magic flowers	76	Ink spots and stripes
55	Floating flowers	78	Bouncing bugs
56	Climbing lizard	80	Monster in the city drawing
58	Swirly spinner	82	Spinning paper helicopter
60	Magic monster heads	84	Bendy balancers
61	Fishing game	86	Light catcher
62	Fantastic flingers	88	Floating water beastie
64	Tricks of the eye	89	Soap-powered fish
66	Squirty whale	90	Catapult plane
68	City skyline	92	Blow-painted monster
69	Triangle tower	93	Oozing slime
70	Tasty bread rolls	94	Websites to visit
		96	Index

About this book

These two pages tell you about some of the things you'll need for the activities in this book. To help you, there's also a YOU WILL NEED list at the start of every project.

At the back of the book there are two pages of science websites where you can find out fun and fascinating facts, and things to do at home too.

Beads and buttons

Large clips and paperclips

Around the house

Most of the projects use things that you might find around your house, such as poster tack, plastic food bags, bottles, plastic containers and lots more.

Marker pens and felt-tip pens

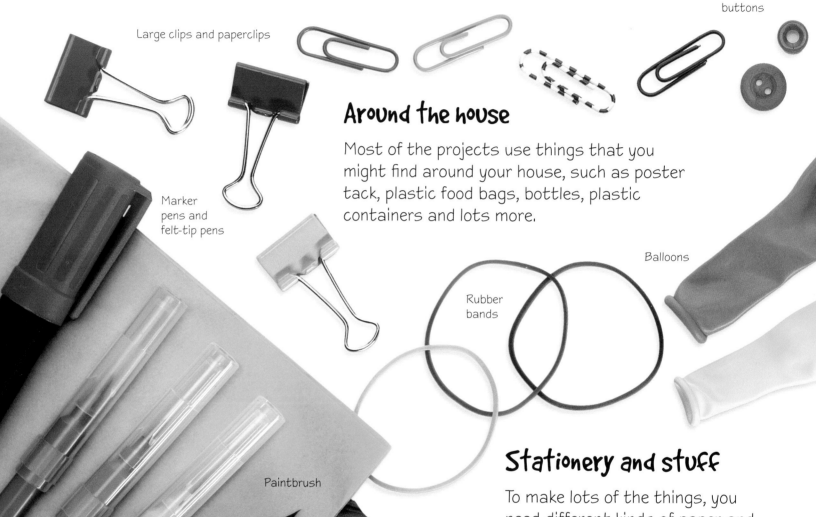

Balloons

Rubber bands

Paintbrush

Paper and cardboard

Stationery and stuff

To make lots of the things, you need different kinds of paper and cardboard. You can decorate what you've made with stickers from the middle of the book, but you may also need pens, pencils and paints, or glitter and sequins.

Wax crayons

Chalk pastels

Sequins

Arts and crafts

Lots of projects use things such as pipe cleaners, buttons and ribbons. If you don't already have these, you can buy them from an arts and crafts store or a haberdashery department.

Pipe cleaners and drinking straws

Dried beans

Kitchen foil

In the kitchen

You'll need ingredients for some of the projects, but you can find lots of other useful things in the kitchen too. Foil, satay sticks and food dye are just some of the things you might find.

Leaves for printing

Toothpicks and satay sticks

Food dye

5

If you make the bubbling brew in a bottle, make sure you use one with a wide neck.

Tiny gold star confetti was added to this jar, to make the brew look really magical.

Bubbling wizard's brew

YOU WILL NEED: a clean glass jar, clear vinegar, food dye, glitter, washing-up liquid, bicarbonate of soda

Don't put a lid on the jar.

1. Half-fill a glass jar with clear vinegar. Add several drops of food dye, then sprinkle a little glitter over the top of the vinegar.

2. Add a good squeeze of washing-up liquid to the jar. Then, gently stir the mixture with a metal spoon to mix everything together.

3. Put the jar in the middle of a large baking tray or a sink. Add a heaped teaspoon of bicarbonate of soda to the jar and see what happens.

Foaming brew

The foam that pours out of the jar is formed by a simple chemical reaction. When the vinegar and bicarbonate of soda mix, they make lots of tiny bubbles of gas. The bubbles churn up the washing-up liquid, making lots of foam.

The wizard's brew is not a drink, so don't drink it.

Zappy zoomer

YOU WILL NEED: cardboard, drinking straws

You need to be able to bend the cardboard, but it still needs to be fairly strong.

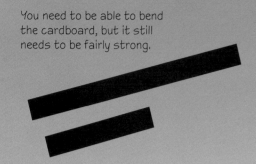

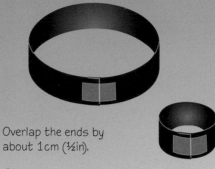

Overlap the ends by about 1cm (½in).

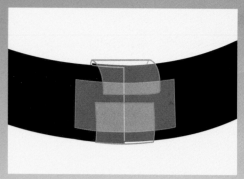

1. Cut a cardboard strip that is 2.5 x 24cm (1 x 9½in) in size. Then, cut a second strip that is the same width, but only 12cm (5in) long.

2. To make the strips into round loops, press a piece of sticky tape onto one end of each strip. Overlap the ends, then press down the tape.

3. To make the joins in the loops stronger, cut two longer pieces of sticky tape. Wrap one piece around the join in each loop, like this.

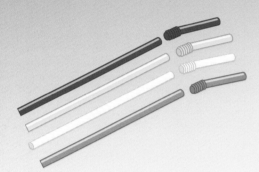

4. To make the sides of the zoomer, cut off the bendy part of four drinking straws. The straight pieces of straw should all be the same length.

You could make a zoomer with three straws, like this one — it will still fly well!

8

Flying high

The zoomer flies because it is light and cuts through the air. Smooth, streamlined shapes allow air to flow around them easily. Planes and cars are designed like this — the more streamlined they are, the faster they can go.

Tape the straws on like this...

... then like this.

5. Tape the end of one straw to the inside of the larger cardboard loop. Then, tape a second straw opposite the first one, like this.

6. Tape the ends of the straws to the outside of the smaller loop. Tape the last straws between the first two, so that they are evenly spaced.

7. To make the zoomer fly, pick it up with the smaller loop facing forward. Hold it by the straw at the bottom, then throw it hard.

Fingerprint fun

YOU WILL NEED: a kitchen sponge cloth and thick paint (poster paint is best)

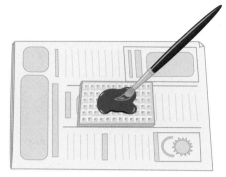

If the paint is too sticky to make a good print, dab water on your finger.

1. Cut a piece from a kitchen sponge cloth and lay it on an old newspaper. Brush thick paint onto part of the sponge, so that it soaks in a little.

2. Press the end of one of your fingers into the paint. Press it into the paint a few times, until the end of your finger is covered with paint.

3. Press your finger onto a piece of paper to make a print. You may get a clearer print if you press your finger onto the paper a second time.

Make prints of all your fingers and both your thumbs using different paints.

Draw arms, legs, faces and clothes on your prints, to make them into cartoons.

Printing press

The skin on the ends of your fingers has tiny ridges in it. These ridges form patterns that you can see when you make a fingerprint. Here are some patterns to look for:

whorl   arch   loop

The red prints were made using an ink stamp pad instead of paint.

Detective work

YOU WILL NEED: chalk or a chalk pastel and clear sticky tape

Don't move your finger or the print will smudge.

1. Press a finger onto a clean mirror, or other glass surface. Grease from your skin will stay on the surface when you lift your finger off.

You need about half a teaspoon of powder.

2. Hold a pair of scissors with the blades together. Scrape them down a piece of chalk over a plate, so that the chalk powder falls onto it.

The powder sticks to the fingerprint.

3. Dip a small, dry brush into the powder. Carefully dust lots of chalk powder onto the fingerprint. Then, gently blow off any excess powder.

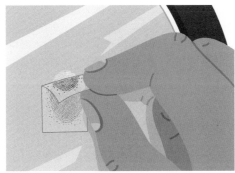

4. To lift the fingerprint off the mirror, carefully lay a piece of clear sticky tape onto the print. Press the tape flat, then peel it off.

Catching criminals

Every fingerprint is different. This means that fingerprints can be used to catch criminals. Forensic scientists lift prints from a crime scene and check them against criminal records. If they find a match, then they know that person was at the crime scene.

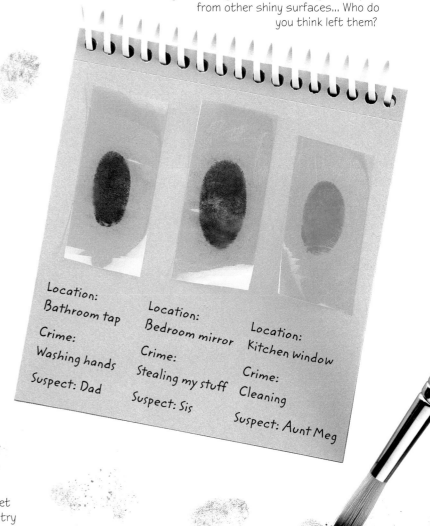

You could go around your house and try to lift prints from other shiny surfaces... Who do you think left them?

Location: Bathroom tap
Crime: Washing hands
Suspect: Dad

Location: Bedroom mirror
Crime: Stealing my stuff
Suspect: Sis

Location: Kitchen window
Crime: Cleaning
Suspect: Aunt Meg

If you can't get a good print, try pressing your finger onto your forehead, then making a print.

Blow on the back of the sail to make the car whoosh forward.

Sail cars

YOU WILL NEED: thin cardboard, two pipe cleaners, three bendy drinking straws, big beads, toothpicks, small beads

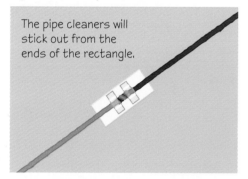

The pipe cleaners will stick out from the ends of the rectangle.

1. Cut a 5 x 11cm (2 x 4in) rectangle of thin cardboard. Twist together the ends of two pipe cleaners, then tape them onto the rectangle.

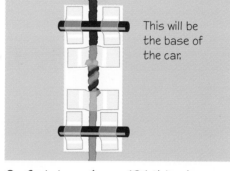

This will be the base of the car.

2. Cut two 6cm (2½in) pieces from a drinking straw. Then, tape the straws across the rectangle, over the pipe cleaners, like this.

Push the pencil a little way into the paper.

3. Cut a square paper sail the length of the bottom part of a bendy straw. Use a sharp pencil to make a hole at the top and bottom of the sail.

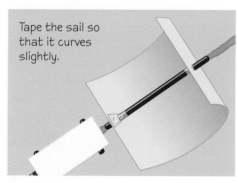

Tape the sail so that it curves slightly.

4. Cut the top off the bendy straw to make a tall mast. Slide the sail on and tape it in place. Slide the mast onto one of the pipe cleaners.

5. Push a big bead onto the pipe cleaner and twist the end. Then, cut an 11cm (4in) piece from another straw and slide it onto the other pipe cleaner.

You may need to trim the end of the pipe cleaner.

6. Bend the mast and short straw over the top of the base. Twist the end of the pipe cleaner around the middle of the mast to hold it in place.

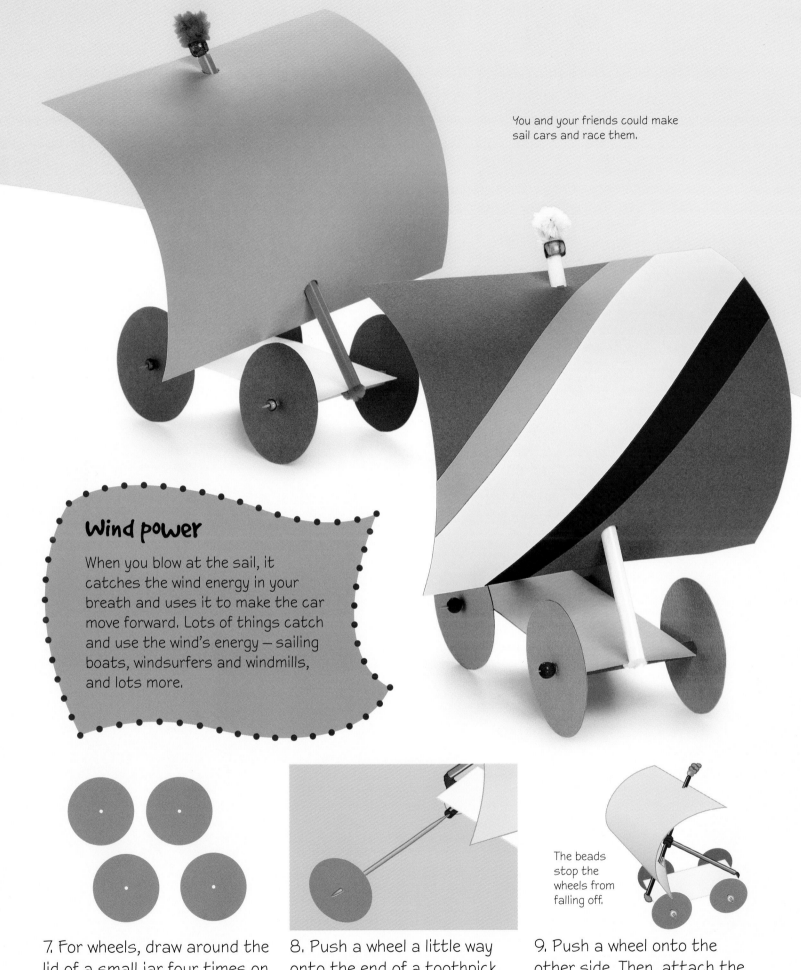

You and your friends could make sail cars and race them.

Wind power

When you blow at the sail, it catches the wind energy in your breath and uses it to make the car move forward. Lots of things catch and use the wind's energy — sailing boats, windsurfers and windmills, and lots more.

The beads stop the wheels from falling off.

7. For wheels, draw around the lid of a small jar four times on cardboard. Cut out the circles and make a hole in the middle of each one with a pin.

8. Push a wheel a little way onto the end of a toothpick. Then, slide the toothpick through one of the straws on the bottom of the car.

9. Push a wheel onto the other side. Then, attach the other wheels in the same way. Push a small bead onto the end of each toothpick.

Spooky shadow puppets

YOU WILL NEED: thick paper, a drinking straw, a torch or desk light

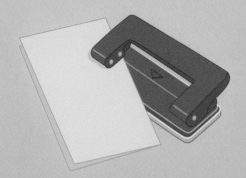

1. Fold a piece of thick paper in half. Push the fold into one side of a hole punch. Punch a hole for an eye about a third of the way down the paper.

2. Draw a mouth with pointed teeth against the fold, like this. Then, keeping the paper folded, cut out the mouth. Unfold the paper.

3. Draw a monster's body coming up from the bottom of the paper. Add horns, then draw the monster's arms and a pointed tail.

Use the ideas on these pages to make different kinds of monsters.

On page 86 you can find out how other materials act when held against a light.

This works best in a dark room.

4. Cut out the monster and tape a straw onto the body for a handle. Then, hold a torch or angle a desk light, so that light shines onto a wall.

5. Hold the puppet in front of the light to cast a shadow on the wall. What happens if you move the puppet away from the light, or tilt it or twist it?

The monster below is symmetrical. Find out more about symmetry on page 33.

Casting shadows

When you hold the puppet in front of the torch or desk light, it stops some of the light from reaching the wall and casts a dark shadow on the wall. Moving the puppet closer to the light makes the shadow bigger, because the puppet is blocking more of the light. Tilting and twisting the puppet changes how it blocks the light, so it changes the shape of the shadow, too.

You could decorate your monster puppet like the one below.

15

Mystery meeting map

YOU WILL NEED: a piece of pale paper which will fit inside your oven, bicarbonate of soda, water, an oven

You will be drawing a route on your map with invisible ink that only appears when it is baked.

You might want to go to the movies.

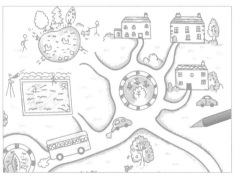

1. You can use this mystery map to arrange to meet a friend. First draw your house on a piece of pale paper. You will add a secret route later.

2. Draw the roads around where you live. Then, draw the place where you want to meet. Add houses and landmarks along the route.

3. Draw trees, cars and buses on your map, then add some people, too. Shade in your drawing and add grass around the roads.

If you're having a party, you can use the mystery map as a fun invitation. Draw a map, then make copies of it using a photocopier or scanner. Use the bicarbonate of soda to show your friends where to meet you, then send the invitations. Remember to tell them how to reveal the route!

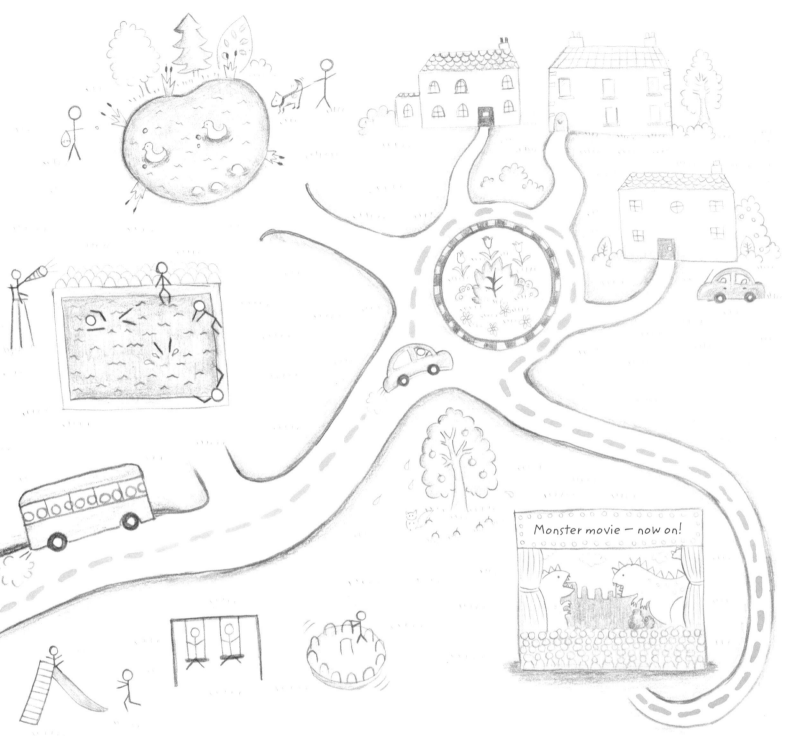

The route won't show until it is baked.

4. To mark the secret route, mix 1 teaspoon of bicarbonate of soda with 2 tablespoons of water in a glass. Brush on the route using a thin paintbrush.

Use oven mitts to put the map into the oven and to lift it out.

5. Give the map to your friend. Tell them to heat an oven to 150°C, 300°F, gas mark 2 and bake the map for 10 minutes to make the route appear.

Invisible ink

People have written secret messages with invisible inks for hundreds of years. But how does the 'ink' in this project work? When you heat the map in the oven, you trigger a chemical reaction between the paper and the bicarbonate of soda. This reaction causes the places that were brushed with ink to turn brown.

Bobbing bouncing raisins

YOU WILL NEED: an unopened bottle of clear fizzy lemonade, a tall glass, raisins, sultanas or currants (small ones work best)

1. Carefully unscrew the lid of a bottle of lemonade and take it off. Pour the lemonade into a tall glass, until the glass is about three-quarters full.

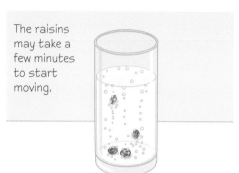

The raisins may take a few minutes to start moving.

2. Drop several raisins into the lemonade, then watch to see what happens. The raisins will sink to the bottom, then start to float to the surface.

The raisins should keep bobbing up and down for a couple of hours.

3. Keep watching the raisins. Each time they float to the surface, they will stay there for a moment, then sink down to the bottom again.

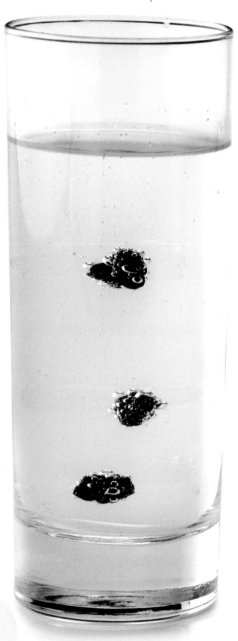

Bursting bubbles

Fizzy drinks are crammed with lots of tiny bubbles of a gas called carbon dioxide. The bubbles are lighter than the liquid they're in, so they float up to the surface. When you drop raisins into the lemonade, lots of bubbles stick onto them, and carry them up to the surface. When some of the bubbles burst, the raisins sink down again and start to collect more bubbles, before bobbing up again.

You could stir a couple of drops of food dye into the lemonade.

Layered liquids

YOU WILL NEED: cold water, food dye, vegetable oil, a small clean glass jar, golden syrup

1. Half-fill a glass with cold water and add a few drops of food dye. Then, stir the water with a teaspoon, to mix in the food dye.

Try to add the water down the side of the jar.

2. Spoon four tablespoons of vegetable oil into a small glass jar. Then, slowly add four tablespoons of dyed water and see what happens.

3. Slowly add four tablespoons of golden syrup to the jar with a spoon. Then, watch to see what happens to the three liquids in the jar.

What do you think happens if you add the liquids in a different order?

Lots of layers

In your jar, you'll see three layers. Oil is less dense than water, so it floats in a layer on top of it. Syrup is more dense than water and oil, so it sinks through them to form a layer at the bottom.

Sparkly space picture

YOU WILL NEED: plain paper, black paper, gold glitter, shiny paper, glitter glue

1. Fold a piece of paper in half. Then, draw a shape like this against the fold, for the nose of a rocket. Keep the paper folded and cut out the shape.

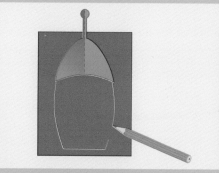

2. Lay the nose on a piece of paper and draw the body of a rocket below it. Cut out the shape, then glue the body onto a piece of black paper.

Tip the paper to get rid of any excess glitter.

3. Glue the nose on so that the fold stands up a little. Then, draw flames and brush white glue over them. Thickly sprinkle glitter over the glue.

4. Cut out an engine and glue it onto the bottom of the rocket. For a window, cut out a paper circle and a smaller circle from shiny paper or foil.

5. Glue the plain circle onto the rocket with the shiny circle on top. Cut out a door and glue it on. Dot glitter glue on the window and door for bolts.

6. Cut out two fins and glue them onto the sides of the rocket. Then, cut out three big flames and glue them on top of the glittery ones.

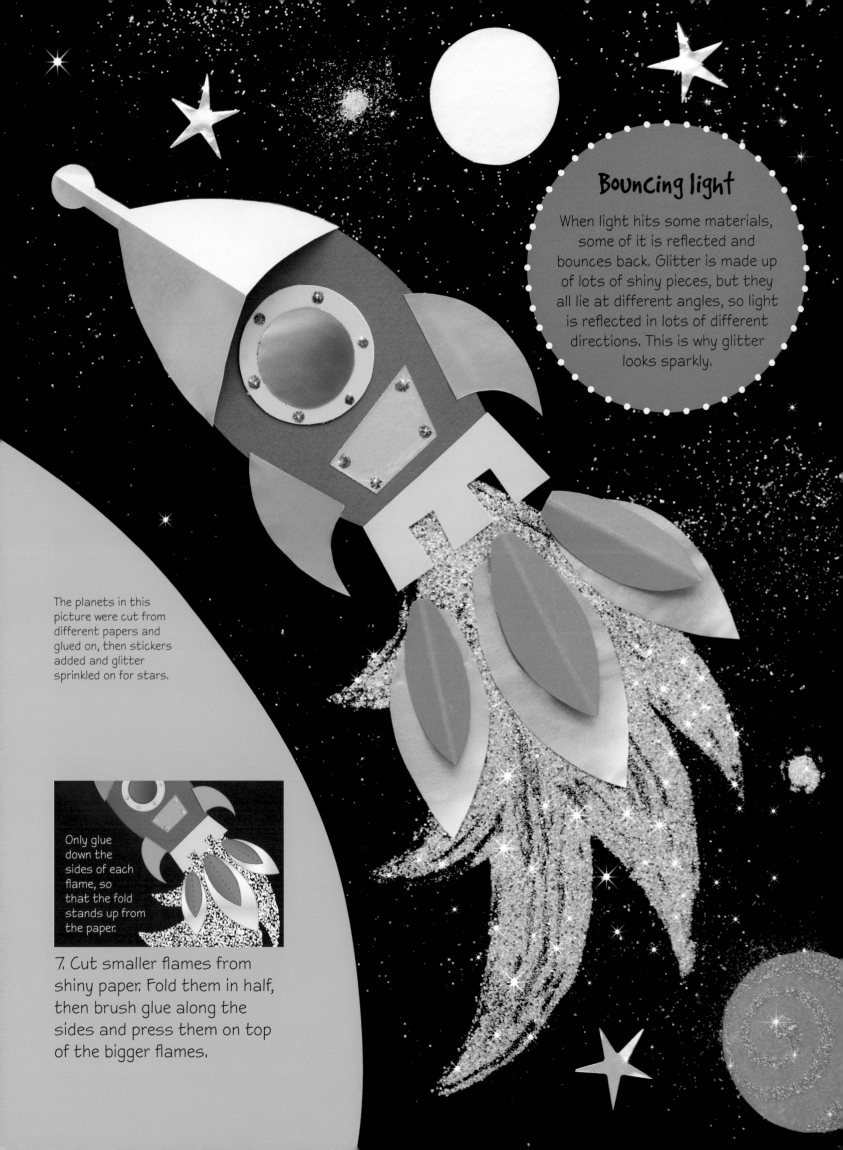

Bouncing light

When light hits some materials, some of it is reflected and bounces back. Glitter is made up of lots of shiny pieces, but they all lie at different angles, so light is reflected in lots of different directions. This is why glitter looks sparkly.

The planets in this picture were cut from different papers and glued on, then stickers added and glitter sprinkled on for stars.

Only glue down the sides of each flame, so that the fold stands up from the paper.

7. Cut smaller flames from shiny paper. Fold them in half, then brush glue along the sides and press them on top of the bigger flames.

Beany bags

YOU WILL NEED: dried black-eyed beans, a small self-sealing plastic food bag, a kitchen sponge cloth

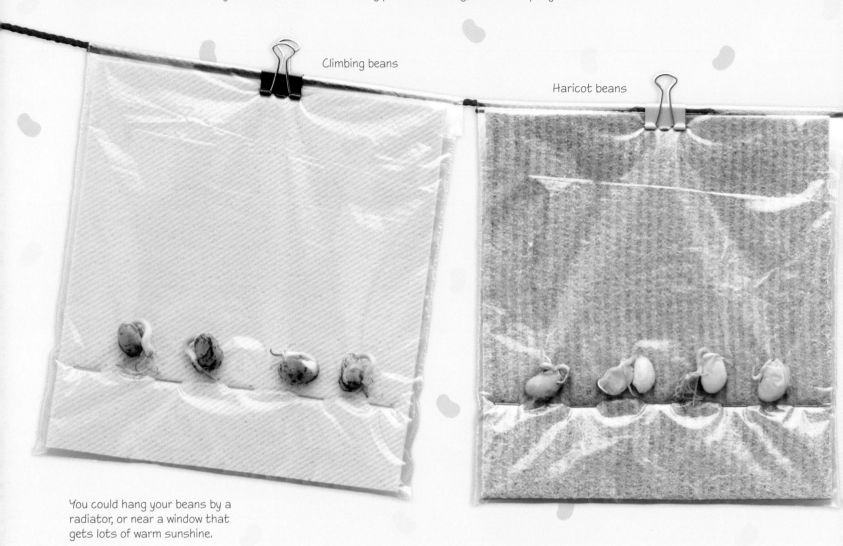

Climbing beans

Haricot beans

You could hang your beans by a radiator, or near a window that gets lots of warm sunshine.

Soak the beans the day before you want to start growing them.

1. Fill a glass with cold water. Put three or four black-eyed beans into the glass and leave them to soak for 24 hours. Then, lift them out.

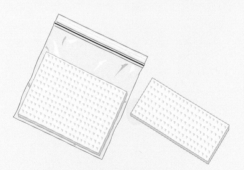

2. Lay a small self-sealing food bag flat and lay a sponge cloth on it. Then, cut the sponge so that it will fit inside the bag.

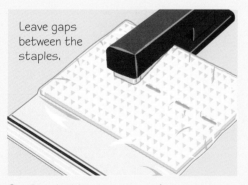

Leave gaps between the staples.

3. Push the sponge into the bag so that it rests in the bottom. Then, staple a line of about five staples part way down the sponge.

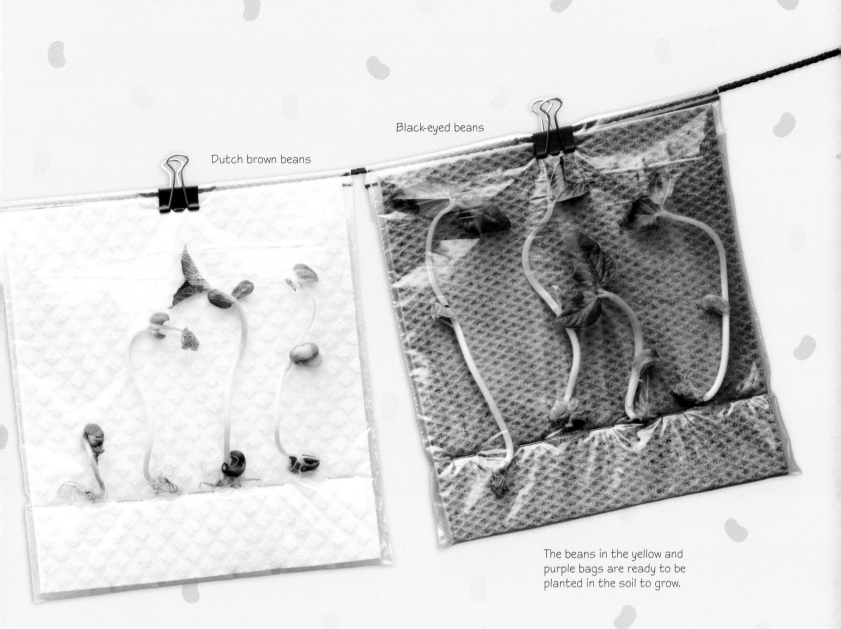

Dutch brown beans

Black-eyed beans

The beans in the yellow and purple bags are ready to be planted in the soil to grow.

Not all beans grow at the same rate, so try experimenting with different kinds.

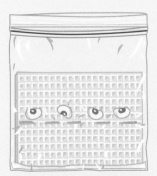

4. Add four tablespoons of water to wet the sponge. Then, put the beans into the bag, so that they are resting on the line of staples.

If the sponge starts to dry out, add a little water, then reseal the bag.

5. Seal the bag, keeping some air inside it, then put the bag in a warm dry place. Check the beans every day to see what happens.

Food for growth

Beans are seeds and they are full of all the food that a plant needs to start growing. When they are given water, air and warmth, they start to germinate, or grow. They sprout white roots and green stems, then grow leaves. Once the beans have leaves, they also need light. The leaves then absorb energy from the light in a process called photosynthesis.

floating ball game

YOU WILL NEED: thick paper, a bendy drinking straw, poster tack, foil

Tape the edges on the inside and outside of the cone.

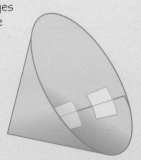

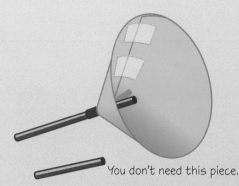

You don't need this piece.

You could decorate the cone with stickers from this book.

1. Draw around a mug on thick paper, then cut out the circle. Make a cut into the middle, then bend the sides around to make a cone. Tape the edges.

2. Cut a small piece off the point of the cone. Push the short end of a bendy straw into the hole. Then, cut a piece off the bottom of the straw.

Press the poster tack onto the cone to hold the straw in place.

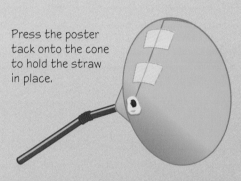

3. Press poster tack around the end of the straw. Then, slide the straw down until the poster tack is resting in the bottom of the cone, like this.

Try blowing through the straw at different speeds. What happens to the ball?

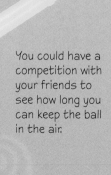

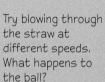

Blow into the end of the straw.

You could have a competition with your friends to see how long you can keep the ball in the air.

4. Scrunch a piece of foil into a ball that is about the size of a cherry. Put the ball in the cone. Bend the end of the straw and blow through it.

High pressure

When you blow through the straw, a jet of air whooshes up under the foil ball. This high pressure jet sends the ball up into the air. As the air flows up the sides of the cone, it spreads out and loses pressure. The foil ball bounces about as it hits the high and low air pressures above the cone.

24

Head to head

YOU WILL NEED: thick papers, pencils, thread

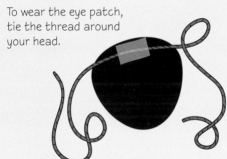

To wear the eye patch, tie the thread around your head.

Hold one rhino in each hand.

1. Draw a rhino on a piece of yellow paper, then draw one facing the other way on purple paper. Draw faces on them, then cut them out.

2. For an eye patch, draw a rounded shape on thick paper, then cut it out. Cut a long piece of thread, then tape it to the back of the eye patch.

3. Put on your eye patch. Pick up the rhinos, and try to make their horns touch, like this. Then, take off the eye patch and try again.

Hit and miss

Wearing an eye patch, it's hard to touch the rhinos together, but when you take it off, it's easy to do. This is because eyes work in pairs. Each eye sees the rhinos from a slightly different angle and your brain puts together what they see to make one 3-dimensional image. This means that it can judge how something looks from top to bottom and from side to side, and can work out WHERE it is. If you cover up one eye, your brain finds it harder to work out where things are because it is only sent one image.

Tropical reef painting

YOU WILL NEED: wax crayons, thick paper, watery paints

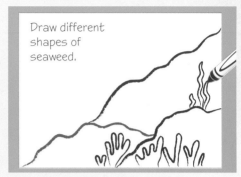
Draw different shapes of seaweed.

1. Use a dark wax crayon to draw rocks on a big piece of thick, white paper. Add seaweed growing on some of the rocks.

2. Draw different corals on some of the rocks, using bright wax crayons. Then, draw circles inside some of the bigger corals.

3. Draw outlines of lots of different kinds of tropical fish swimming around the rocks. Then, draw stripes and spots on the fish.

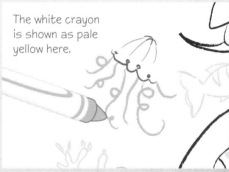
The white crayon is shown as pale yellow here.

4. Use a white crayon to draw a curved shape for the top of a jellyfish. Add a pink wavy line underneath, then draw long pale tendrils.

5. Draw lots of white bubbles. Then, use pale blue watery paint to fill in the sea around the fish. The crayon lines will resist the paint.

6. Fill in the rocks using watery paints. Then, fill in the coral, seaweed and the fish and jellyfish. When the paint is dry, add eyes on the fish.

Look at this picture for ideas of what to put in your painting.

watertight wax

The crayon lines resist the watery paint because they contain wax. Wax is waterproof, which means that it repels water, like a raincoat. Unlike wax, the paper is not waterproof, so it doesn't resist the paint at all.

Dangly monkeys

YOU WILL NEED: thick paper, felt-tip pens, pipe cleaners, thread

1. Fold a piece of thick paper in half, then in half again. Draw a monkey's head, ears and body on the paper. Add an arm curving up over the head.

2. Draw the other arm curving down, then add legs and a long tail. Cut out the monkey through all the layers of paper. This will make four monkeys.

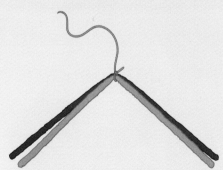

3. Turn one or two monkeys over, then decorate them all using felt-tip pens. Then, add the monkeys' faces using a thin black pen.

4. Bend two pipe cleaners in half and pinch the middle. Then, unbend the pipe cleaners a little and tie a piece of thread around the middle.

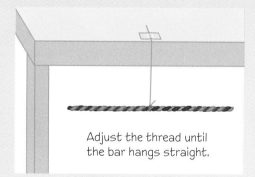

Adjust the thread until the bar hangs straight.

5. Straighten the pipe cleaners, then twist them together to make a bar. Tape the thread onto a table or other surface, like this.

You could make snakes as well as monkeys. They weigh less, so how do you think they will affect the bar?

You could make more than one set of monkeys to hang from your bar.

Seesaw forces

The bar acts like a seesaw, and the thread in the middle is its pivot — the point that it swings around.

Adding a monkey at one end of the bar makes it tilt a lot...

...but the bar only tilts a little with the monkey halfway.

This happens because things far away from the pivot have a bigger force on the bar than things closer to the pivot.

Hanging a monkey from the tail of another also makes the force bigger. This makes the bar swing down more than if there was only one monkey.

6. Hang a monkey at one end of the pipe cleaners. Then, hang another monkey on the other side, halfway along. Does the bar hang straight?

7. Hang another monkey from the tail of the second one. Then, experiment with hanging all the monkeys at different points along the bar.

Melted chocolate circles

TO MAKE ABOUT 12 CIRCLES YOU WILL NEED: 50g of milk chocolate chips and 50g of white chocolate chips

1. Lay a baking tray on a piece of baking parchment and draw around it with a pencil. Cut out the rectangle, then lay it in the baking tray.

2. Put the milk chocolate chips into a small heatproof bowl. Then, put the white chocolate chips into another small heatproof bowl.

3. Fill a large saucepan a quarter full of water and heat it until the water bubbles. Then, carefully remove the pan from the heat.

Use a metal spoon.

4. Wearing oven mitts, carefully put the bowl of milk chocolate chips into the pan. Stir the chocolate until all of the chips have melted.

Wear oven mitts.

Use the back of the spoon.

5. Wearing oven mitts, carefully lift the bowl out of the water. Heat the pan again, until the water bubbles, then remove the pan from the heat.

6. Carefully put the bowl of white chocolate drops into the pan and stir them until they melt. Then, lift the bowl out of the pan again.

7. Spoon a teaspoon of milk chocolate onto the baking parchment. Add five more spoonfuls, then spread each one out to make a circle.

Swirl loops and squiggles in the chocolate.

The chocolate circles need to be eaten within a week.

8. Using another teaspoon, dribble a little white chocolate onto each circle. Then, swirl a toothpick through the chocolate to make patterns.

9. Make six white chocolate circles, then dribble a little milk chocolate onto each one. Swirl the chocolate to make patterns on each circle.

10. Chill the chocolate circles in a refrigerator for 45 minutes, then peel them off the baking parchment. Store them in an airtight container.

Solid-liquid-solid

Chocolate is made up of tiny little particles. At room temperature, it forms a solid shape as all the particles are squashed together. As you heat the chocolate, the particles spread out more and the solid turns into a runny liquid. Then, as it cools, the chocolate turns solid again.

Rocket patterns

YOU WILL NEED: thin cardboard and paper

Add flames to the rockets at the top to make them look like they are launching.

1. Cut a 3 x 4cm (1 x 1½in) rectangle from cardboard. Draw a line down the middle of the rectangle, then add a line across it, halfway down.

2. Cut a corner from the top of the rectangle. Then, keeping the corner the same way up, move it to the bottom of the rectangle and tape it on.

3. Cut off the other top corner in the same way, then tape it to the bottom as well. Then, draw around the shape on several scraps of paper.

You could press on stickers from the sticker pages for windows.

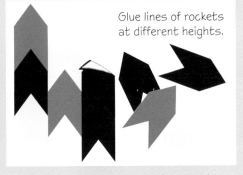

Glue lines of rockets at different heights.

4. Cut out the rockets and glue one onto some paper. Add more rockets above it, with the tails fitting onto the tips. Glue on more lines of rockets.

fitting perfectly

The rockets fit together again and again to make a pattern without any gaps in it. This is called a tessellation. Some shapes tessellate, but others don't. Try cutting other shapes, such as circles, triangles and stars... Do they tessellate?

folded robot

YOU WILL NEED: different shades of paper

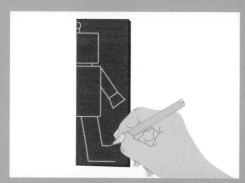

1. Fold a piece of paper in half. Draw half a robot's head, neck and body against the fold. Add an antenna, then draw the robot's arm and a leg.

Keep the paper folded as you cut.

2. Cut out the robot. Draw shapes for an eye and a mouth against the fold, then add shapes on the body. Cut out all the shapes down the fold.

Try to make both halves of the robot look the same.

3. Unfold the robot, then glue it onto a piece of paper. Fold scraps of paper and draw eyes and control panels. Cut them out and glue them on in pairs.

There are pairs of stickers in the middle of this book that you can stick onto your robot, too.

Two halves make a whole

When you unfold the paper, it changes from a meaningless shape into a robot. The robot is symmetrical, which means that each half of the robot is exactly the same, but the opposite way around. Shapes that have different halves are asymmetrical.

Leaf prints

YOU WILL NEED: leaves (they mustn't be dried out) and thick paint

You can store your leaves in a sealed plastic bag in a cool place.

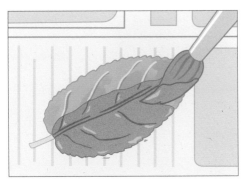

1. Find some fallen leaves, or ask permission to pick some from a garden. It's important to print with leaves that haven't dried up too much.

2. Pour some thick paint onto an old plate. Then, add some water to the paint and mix it in to make the paint slightly runny.

3. Lay a leaf on an old newspaper, with its underside facing up. Brush a thick layer of paint onto the leaf until it is completely covered.

You can see how the veins spread out across the leaf.

4. Lay the leaf on the newspaper with its painted side down. Press the back, to make a print. This will remove excess paint from the leaf.

5. Press the leaf onto a piece of paper to make a clear print. Try making more prints using the other leaves you collected in step 1.

Press all over the back of the leaf to get an even print.

Veiny leaves

Plants have roots that suck up water from the soil. The water flows up the stem, then into the leaves, along tubes called veins. You can clearly see the veins in the leaf prints.

fishbowl spinner

YOU WILL NEED: thick white paper, felt-tip pens, thread

Draw the weeds
up the sides of
the bowl.

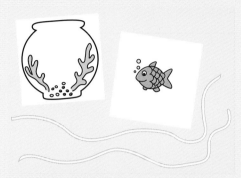

Make the gap about
as wide as your finger.

1. Cut two 10cm (4in) squares of thick white paper. On one of them, draw a fishbowl that almost fills the paper. Add pebbles and weeds.

2. Draw a fish in the middle of the other square. Add a few bubbles coming from its mouth. Then, cut two threads about 30cm (12in) long.

3. Turn the fish picture over, with the picture upside down. Tape the pieces of thread across the back, leaving a gap between them.

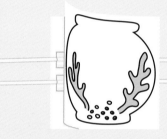

The bowl should be this way up.

Keep flipping the spinner until the threads are completely twisted.

4. Brush white glue over the back of the fishbowl picture. Then, press it onto the back of the upside-down fish picture. Leave the glue to dry.

5. Tightly hold the ends of the threads so that the spinner hangs down. Flip it over and over to twist the threads, then pull the threads tight.

Merging pictures

As the spinner spins, it looks as if the fish is inside the fishbowl. This is because your eyes store a picture of whatever you see for a few seconds after you've seen it. The pictures on the spinner are moving so fast that your eyes see both at once, and your brain merges them to make one picture.

Shark flickbook

YOU WILL NEED: white paper that is thin enough to see through for tracing, a black pen, a stapler

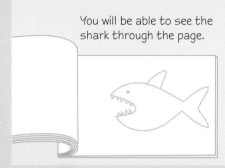
You will be able to see the shark through the page.

The shark could chase a fish, or swish its tail.

1. To make a flickbook, cut fourteen 8 x 5cm (3 x 2in) rectangles from thin white paper. Pile up the rectangles and staple them at one end.

2. Using a black pen, draw a picture of a shark on the back page of the book. Then, turn down the next page, so that it covers the shark.

3. Draw over the outline, but change it a little, so that the shark 'moves' slightly. Then, draw pictures on the other pages in the same way.

4. Hold the flickbook like this, then flick through all the pictures from the back to the front. The shark will look like it's moving.

Shark on the move

As you flick the pages, your eyes and brain blend the pictures, so it looks as if the shark is moving. Some cartoon movies are made like this, but the images move much faster – you see 24 pictures a second, to make the images move smoothly.

Try flicking through the pages at different speeds – does it work best when you go faster or slower?

Swirly snake

YOU WILL NEED: a pipe cleaner, a drinking straw, poster tack, thick paper, pens or stickers for decorating

Don't bend the straw.

1. To make the stand, push a pipe cleaner through a drinking straw, so that one end sticks out of the top. Trim the end so that it is 1cm (½in) long.

A heavy, wide base will make the stand more stable.

2. Press a big blob of poster tack onto a flat surface, for the base. Then, firmly push the bottom of the straw into the poster tack, like this.

Try drawing around different-sized bowls, plates and mugs to make different snakes.

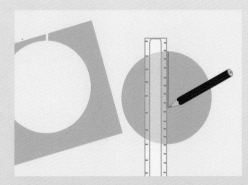

3. For the snake, draw around a small bowl or mug on a piece of thick paper. Cut out the circle, then draw a straight line down the middle of it.

Make sure that the head is in the middle of the circle.

4. Draw another line across the middle of the circle. Draw a shape for the snake's head around where the lines cross, then add a spiral for the body.

You could use stickers from this book to decorate the snake's body.

5. Turn the paper over. Then, draw or stick on spots around the circle. Try not to put spots in the middle of the circle, where the head will be.

38

Glue the tongue onto the back of the head.

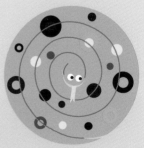

Gently blow the snake to make it swirl around on the stand.

6. Turn the paper over and cut around the spiral and head. Turn the snake over again, then cut out and glue on eyes and a forked tongue.

7. Rest the middle of the snake's head on the top of the pipe cleaner. Move the snake around a little to make it balance perfectly.

Perfectly balanced

Everything on Earth is pulled down to the ground by gravity. As the snake is pulled down, its weight is spread evenly around a point called its centre of gravity. This point is below its head, within the space formed by its body. When you rest the snake on the pipe cleaner, it balances perfectly around its centre of gravity.

39

Mirror magic

YOU WILL NEED: three small mirrors (ones without frames are best), poster tack, paper, paperclips, beads or sequins

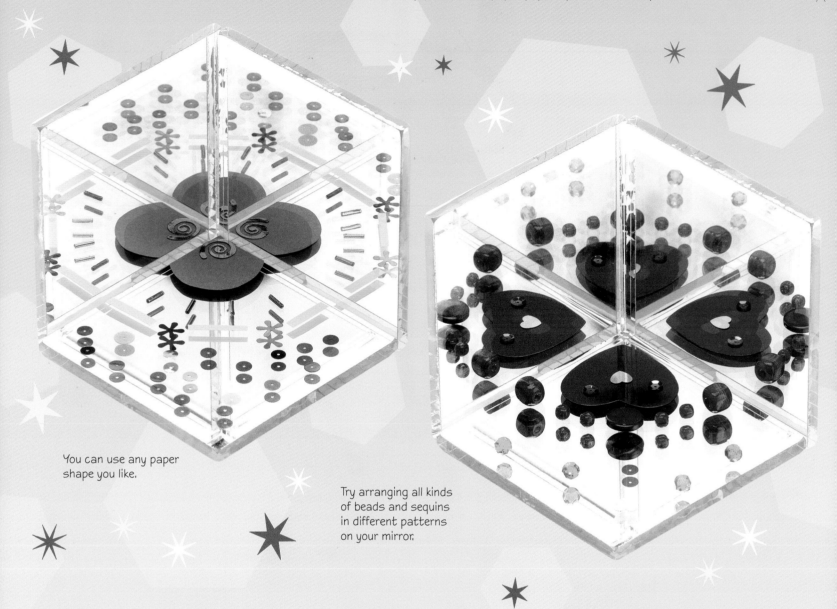

You can use any paper shape you like.

Try arranging all kinds of beads and sequins in different patterns on your mirror.

The balls of poster tack keep the mirror in place.

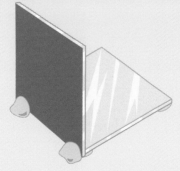

Press the sticky tape onto the back of the mirrors.

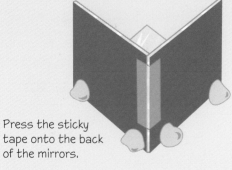

1. Lay a small mirror face down and press a tiny ball of poster tack onto each corner. Then, turn the mirror over and press it onto a flat surface.

2. Push a second small mirror against one edge of the first one. Then, press two bigger balls of poster tack behind the mirror, to keep it upright.

3. Place a third mirror next to the second one and hold it in place with poster tack. Then, tape the edges of the two mirrors together, like this.

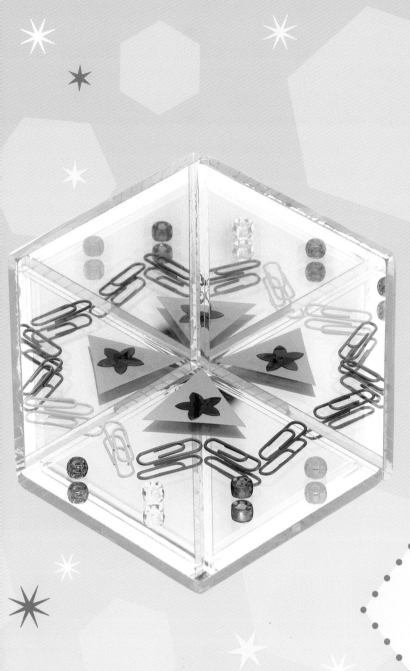

on reflection...

A mirror reflects light so that you can see an image of whatever is in front of it. Arranged like this, the upright mirrors are reflecting each other's images as well as what is on the mirror below. From some angles this makes it look as if there is a fourth mirror 'behind' the others, creating a kaleidoscope effect.

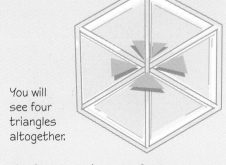

You will see four triangles altogether.

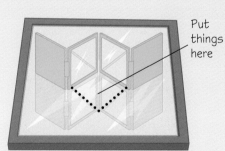

Put things here

If you've got hinged mirrors, bend the backs around, like this.

4. Cut a triangle from paper, then lay it on the bottom mirror. Push it into the corner where the mirrors meet. You will see three reflections.

5. Add paperclips around the triangle, then add beads, too. Try rearranging the things on the mirror, to see how the reflections change.

If you only have two small mirrors, you can still do this project. Place them on top of a big mirror and set them up to make a corner, like this.

41

Lemon slice ice cubes

YOU WILL NEED: a lemon, an ice cube tray, water

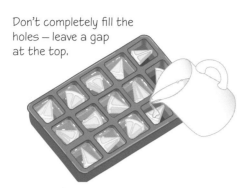

Don't completely fill the holes – leave a gap at the top.

The water will have frozen into ice cubes that fill the holes.

1. Rinse a lemon, then dry it with a paper towel. Lay it on a chopping board, then very carefully cut a couple of slices from it using a sharp knife.

2. Cut each slice in half, then into little wedges. Put one wedge into each hole in a clean ice tray. Then, pour cold water into each hole.

3. Put the ice tray into a freezer and leave it in there overnight. Then, lift out the ice tray. Turn it upside down to push out the ice cubes.

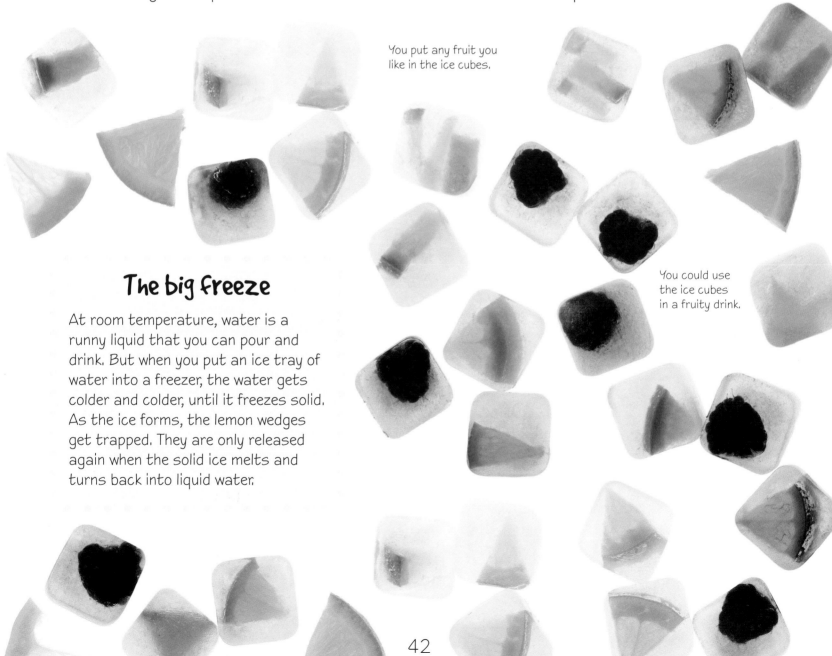

You put any fruit you like in the ice cubes.

You could use the ice cubes in a fruity drink.

The big freeze

At room temperature, water is a runny liquid that you can pour and drink. But when you put an ice tray of water into a freezer, the water gets colder and colder, until it freezes solid. As the ice forms, the lemon wedges get trapped. They are only released again when the solid ice melts and turns back into liquid water.

floating ice boat

YOU WILL NEED: water, food dye, poster tack, a clean dry plastic container, a satay stick, paper, a large bowl of water

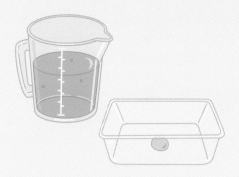

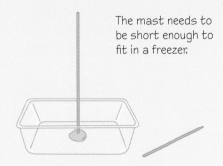

The mast needs to be short enough to fit in a freezer.

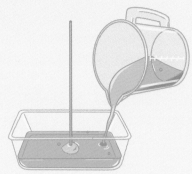

1. Pour cold water into a jug and stir in a few drops of food dye. Then, press a ball of poster tack into the bottom of a dry plastic container.

2. For the ice boat's mast, carefully cut one end off a satay stick. Then, firmly press the stick into the ball of poster tack.

3. Pour the water into the container, until it is about three-quarters full. Put the container into a freezer overnight. Then, lift it out.

You could use stickers from the middle of this book to decorate the sail.

As the ice boat melts, the dye will dissolve into the water.

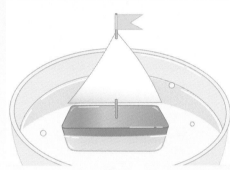

4. Cut a paper sail and push it onto the mast, then cut a flag and glue it on top. Tip the ice boat out of the container and place it in a bowl of cold water.

floating boat

When water freezes, it grows a little, which you may notice when you take the ice boat out of the freezer. Although the ice is bigger, it contains the same amount of water, which means that it is less dense than liquid water. The density of an object is what makes it float or sink, and the ice boat floats because it is less dense than water. What do you think happens to things that are more dense?

43

Flying fish windsock

YOU WILL NEED: thin cardboard, tissue paper, wax crayons, thread, a satay stick

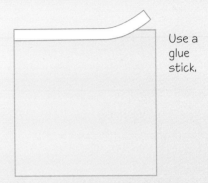

Use a glue stick.

1. Cut a 2.5 x 30cm (1 x 12in) strip from cardboard. Then, cut a 30cm (12in) square from tissue paper and glue the strip along the top.

Try not to rip the tissue paper.

2. Turn the paper over. Then, pressing lightly with a wax crayon, draw a row of fish scales about a third of the way down the paper.

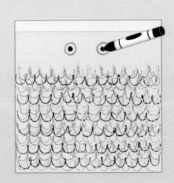

3. Using several different crayons, fill the paper below the first row with overlapping scales. Then, add eyes above them, like this.

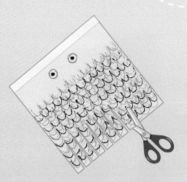

4. For the fish's fluttering tail, make a cut up from the bottom of the paper to halfway up the scales. Then, make lots more cuts.

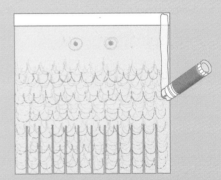

5. Turn the tissue paper over again, so that the scales are facing down. Then, spread glue down one side, stopping before you get to the tail.

6. Bend the cardboard strip into a circle, so that the edges of the tissue paper overlap. Then, hold the glued edges until they stick.

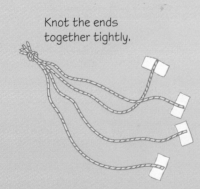

Knot the ends together tightly.

7. Cut four 30cm (12in) pieces of thick thread. Press a piece of sticky tape onto one end of each piece. Then, knot the other ends together.

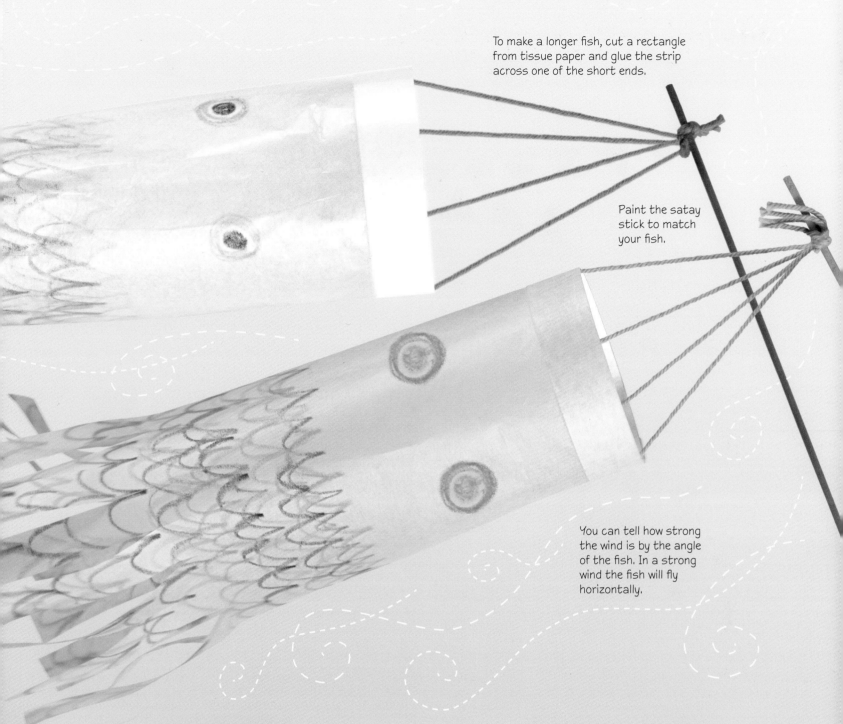

To make a longer fish, cut a rectangle from tissue paper and glue the strip across one of the short ends.

Paint the satay stick to match your fish.

You can tell how strong the wind is by the angle of the fish. In a strong wind the fish will fly horizontally.

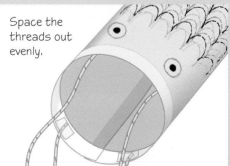

Space the threads out evenly.

8. Tape two of the threads onto the inside of the mouth, one below each eye. Then, tape the other two threads opposite the first two.

Be careful with the pointed end of the stick.

9. Push the pointed end of a satay stick down through the knot in the strings, until only a small part of the stick is left above the knot.

Wind direction

If you hold the windsock outside, it will catch any moving air, or wind. The air blows through the fish's mouth, fills its body and makes the tail move around. Windsocks are used beside airport runways to show pilots the direction and strength of the wind.

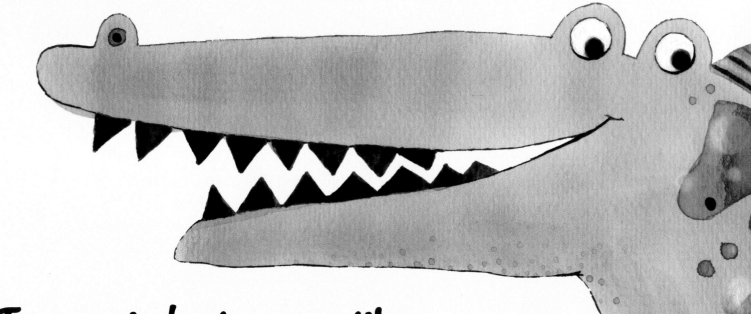

Tea-painted crocodile

YOU WILL NEED: teabags, instant coffee, water, a lemon, pale paper, white paint, a brown pen

Be careful — the water will be very hot.

1. Put eight teabags into a mug. Then, spoon two heaped teaspoons of instant coffee into another mug. Half-fill a kettle, then turn it on.

2. Very carefully, fill the mug of tea with hot water and pour about 2cm (1in) of water into the coffee. Stir the mixtures well, then let them cool.

Don't pour away the tea — you'll use it again in step 6.

3. Carefully cut a lemon in half, using a sharp knife. Then, use a lemon juicer to squeeze the juice out of both halves. Pour the juice into a glass.

4. Take the teabags out of the cold tea, then dip a brush into it. Paint a crocodile's body on pale paper. Add a head with bumps for the eyes and nose.

5. Paint a long curled tail, then add lots of spikes along the crocodile's back. Paint two legs with claws, then leave the tea to dry.

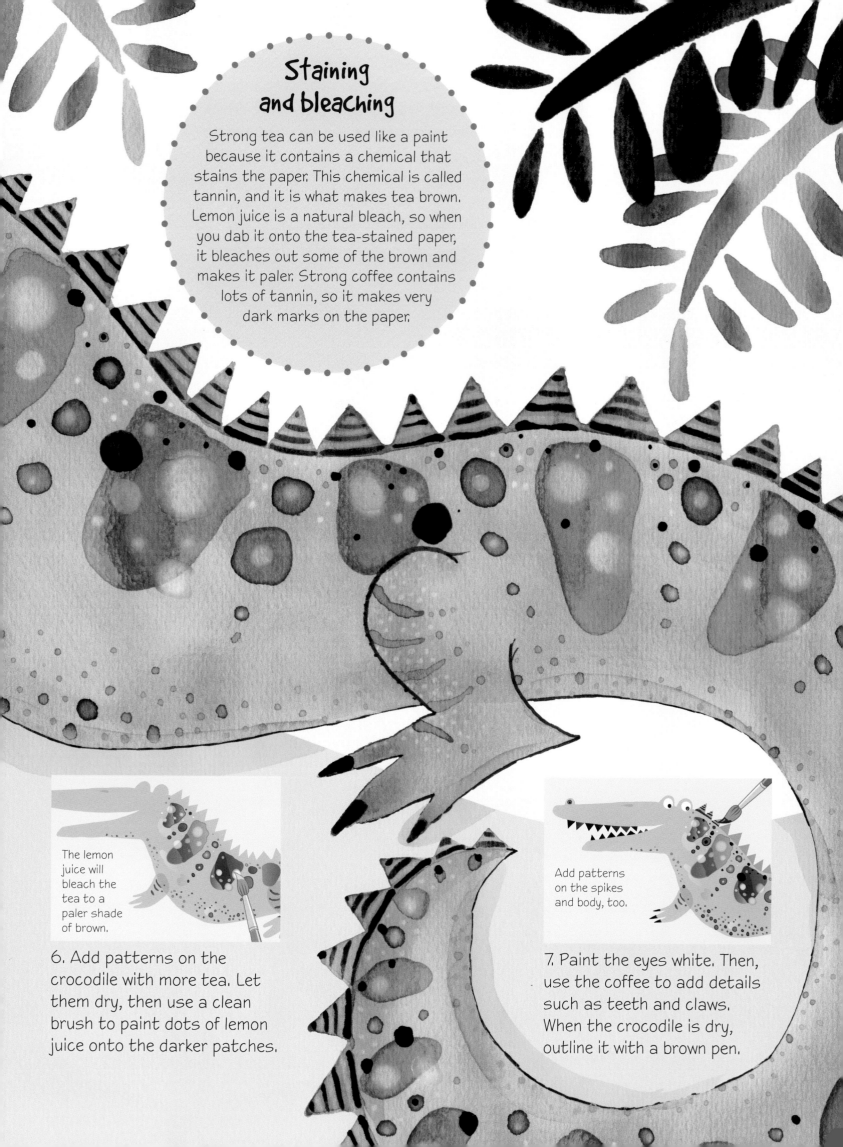

Staining and bleaching

Strong tea can be used like a paint because it contains a chemical that stains the paper. This chemical is called tannin, and it is what makes tea brown. Lemon juice is a natural bleach, so when you dab it onto the tea-stained paper, it bleaches out some of the brown and makes it paler. Strong coffee contains lots of tannin, so it makes very dark marks on the paper.

The lemon juice will bleach the tea to a paler shade of brown.

Add patterns on the spikes and body, too.

6. Add patterns on the crocodile with more tea. Let them dry, then use a clean brush to paint dots of lemon juice onto the darker patches.

7. Paint the eyes white. Then, use the coffee to add details such as teeth and claws. When the crocodile is dry, outline it with a brown pen.

fluttering ghost

YOU WILL NEED: dark paper, white paper, a gold pen, a clean glass bottle

You will use the flap to make the ghost stand up.

You could use a ghost sticker from the middle pages.

1. Cut a 4 x 13cm (1½ x 6in) strip from dark paper, then cut a curve around the top. Fold the bottom of the strip back to make a flap.

2. Draw a little ghost on white paper and cut it out. Glue it near the top of the strip, then add lots of little stars with a gold pen.

Blow at the bottle, not directly at the ghost.

3. Tape the flap onto a surface so that the ghost stands up. Put a bottle about 8cm (3in) away, then blow at the bottle and watch the ghost.

Try moving the ghost around – does this make a difference?

Air on the move

When you blow, your breath hits the curved side of the bottle, splits and goes around both sides. It joins together again on the other side of the bottle, then hits the paper ghost. This is why the ghost flutters, even though the bottle is between you and the ghost.

Zooming balloon rocket

YOU WILL NEED: strong thread, a drinking straw, two chairs, a long balloon, a large clip

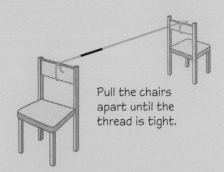

Pull the chairs apart until the thread is tight.

The clip stops the air from escaping.

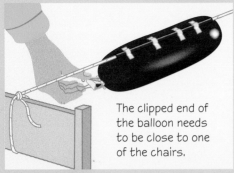

The clipped end of the balloon needs to be close to one of the chairs.

1. Cut a 3m (10ft) piece of thread. Thread it through a drinking straw. Tie each end of the string to the back of a chair, then move them apart.

2. Blow up a long balloon, then twist its end and clip it with a large clip. Using pieces of sticky tape, tape the balloon onto the straw, like this.

3. Carefully pull the straw along to one end of the thread. Then, quickly remove the clip from the end of the balloon and see what happens.

You could decorate your balloon to look like a rocket, using stickers from the middle of this book.

Whooshing air

The air in the balloon is under a lot of pressure and is trying to escape. When you take off the clip, the air rushes out, pushing the balloon in the opposite direction.

Rock and roll eggs

YOU WILL NEED: two eggs, a marble, poster tack, tissue paper

You don't need the egg white or yolk.*

1. Tap the middle of an egg sharply on the rim of a mug to crack it. Use your fingers to carefully break the egg in half over the mug.

2. Break a second egg in half, then wash both the eggshells. Leave them to dry, then put a marble into the bottom half of one of the shells.

3. Using white glue, glue a ball of poster tack into the bottom half of the other shell. Then, leave the glue to dry completely.

* You could use the whites and yolks for cooking.

Use the ideas shown here for different ways to decorate your eggs.

Match the edges as well as you can.

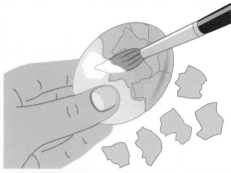

4. To put the eggs back together, rip several short strips from tissue paper. Then, quickly brush all the strips with white glue.

5. Hold the bottom of one of the eggshells and gently lay the other half on top. Press the glue-covered tissue strips over the join.

6. Rip more tissue paper into lots of small pieces. Brush part of the egg with glue, then press pieces of tissue paper onto the glue.

Cover the second egg with a different shade of tissue paper.

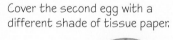
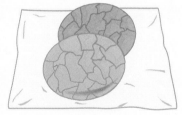

Use stickers from this book for faces.

7. Cover the rest of the egg with tissue paper. Then, cover the other egg in the same way, and put both eggs on plastic foodwrap to dry.

8. Paint patterns and faces on the eggs, then let the paint dry. Then, put the eggs on a table and try pushing them over — what do they do?

Heavy bottoms

Why do you think that one egg rolls and the other one pops back up? It's because each egg moves until its heaviest part (the marble or poster tack) is as close as possible to the ground.

The marble can roll around inside the egg, staying close to the ground all the time. As the marble rolls the egg rolls with it until the marble stops moving.

The poster tack is glued on and can't roll around. When you push the egg, it falls over, but its heavy bottom makes it rock back up again.

Watery whale painting

YOU WILL NEED: thick white paper, black ink, water

These groups of fish were painted using different dilutions of watery paint.

52

1. Using a pencil, draw a whale's body, tail and fin on a piece of thick white paper. Then, add a line for its jaw, flipper and belly, like this.

2. For the markings, draw a long thin shape along the side of the whale. Then, add a small half-circle above the whale's jaw.

3. Carefully pour some black ink onto an old plate. Then, use a thin paintbrush to fill in the whale's body and tail. Don't paint the markings yet.

You could cut out your whale and glue it onto a salt-painted background like this one. (You can find out more about salt painting on pages 72-73.)

4. To dilute the ink and make it a little paler, mix in some water, then test it on a scrap of paper. Then, fill in one of the markings on the whale's body.

5. Mix some more water into the ink to make it even paler. Fill in the rest of the whale, then leave the ink to dry. Add an eye with a black pen.

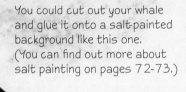

Lighter and lighter

The ink is crammed with lots of tiny particles that make it look black. When you mix in water, the ink particles scatter and spread out among the water particles. The way the ink spreads out in the water is called dilution. Because the gaps between the particles are bigger, the liquid looks paler.

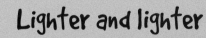

Magic flowers

YOU WILL NEED: a white carnation flower, a clean clear vase or glass, food dye or ink

1. Take the leaves off the stem of a carnation and leave it out of water for an hour. Then, pour 150ml (5fl oz) of water into a vase or glass.

The flower needs to be able to stand upright in the glass or vase.

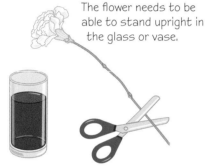

2. Mix one teaspoon of food dye or ink into the water. Cut off the end of the flower stem, then put the flower in the water. Leave it for a few hours.

Sucking up

Inside a flower's stem there are thin tubes that help it to suck up water. When you put a flower in water, the water is drawn up the inside of these tubes. As the water is drawn up, it pulls up more water from below. The veins in this flower's petals start to change as the dyed water reaches them, then become darker and darker as more water is drawn up.

These flowers were dyed with different inks.

After a few days the flower stops sucking up water. Throw it away when it wilts.

Floating flowers

YOU WILL NEED: paper and a bowl

Cut along the lines through the layers of paper.

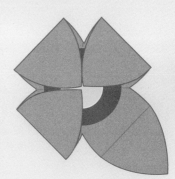

1. Cut out a square of paper. Fold the paper in half, then in half again. Draw a petal shape coming from the folded corner, then cut it out.

2. Open out the paper. Then, fold the tip of each petal into the middle, like this. Crease each fold well, then unfold the flower again.

3. Cut paper circles for the middle. Glue them onto the flower, and fold over the petals. Fill a bowl with water, then place the flower on the water.

You could make flowers from different types of paper.

Flowers made from very absorbent paper will open quickly, but thicker, less absorbent paper will open more slowly.

Soaking in

Paper is absorbent, which means that water can soak into it. As the flower absorbs the water, the tiny strands that make up the paper swell. They push out as they grow, forcing the paper petals to open.

Climbing Lizard

YOU WILL NEED: thin cardboard, felt-tip pens, thick thread or string, a straw, a small coin, beads

1. Draw a lizard's head near the top of a piece of thin cardboard. Then, add big round eyes, dots for nostrils and a mouth.

The lizard should be about as long as your hand.

2. Draw two curved lines for the sides of the lizard's body. Add a spiral for the tail at the bottom of one of the lines. Then, add four feet.

3. Draw a spiky spine down the lizard's back, then fill in the lizard with felt-tip pens. Then, carefully cut around it with scissors.

4. Cut a piece of thread or string, about 1m (3ft) long. Then, cut two pieces from a straw, making each piece about 3cm (1in) long.

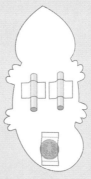

The weight of the coin will help the lizard to work better when you use it.

5. Turn the lizard over and tape the pieces of straw about halfway down. Then, tape a small coin near the bottom, like this.

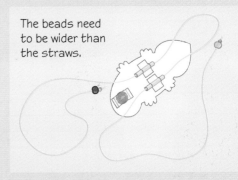

The beads need to be wider than the straws.

6. Push the thread up through one straw, then down through the other one, to make a loop at the top. Thread beads onto the ends and knot them.

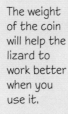
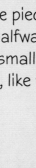

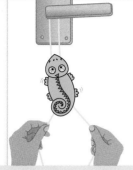

As you pull the threads, pull them out to the side.

7. Loop the middle of the thread over a door handle. To make the lizard climb, pull one end of the thread, then pull the other, again and again.

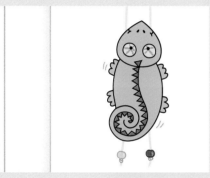

8. When the lizard has climbed up to the door handle, let go of both ends of the thread. The lizard will slide back down to the bottom again.

Up and down

When you pull the threads, they press against the inside of the straws. This creates a force called friction that stops the two things from sliding past each other. When you let go of the threads, they stop pressing against the straws, so there is less friction and the lizard slides down. If you turn your lizard over, you can see this happening.

You could make a climbing bug or spider in the same way.

Swirly spinner

YOU WILL NEED: thin cardboard, felt-tip pens, a rubber band, thread or thin ribbon, beads and buttons

1. Draw around a plate on thin cardboard and cut it out. Then, draw a straight line down the middle of the circle, and another line across it.

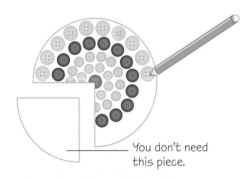

You don't need this piece.

2. Using the lines as a guide, cut out a quarter of the circle. Then, turn the spinner over and decorate the bigger piece with felt-tip pens.

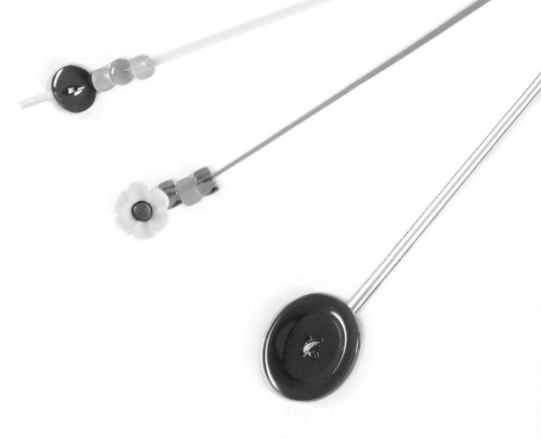

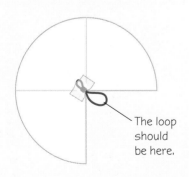

The loop should be here.

3. Tightly tie a knot in one end of a thin rubber band. Turn the circle over and lay the knot in the middle, like this. Press a piece of tape over the knot.

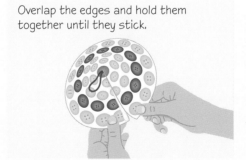

Overlap the edges and hold them together until they stick.

4. Spread glue along one of the straight edges. Bend the circle around with the loop coming out of the top, then press the edges together.

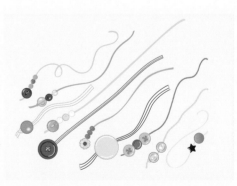

5. Cut ten different lengths of ribbon or thread. Tie a button or bead onto the end of each piece. Then, thread a few more beads onto some of them.

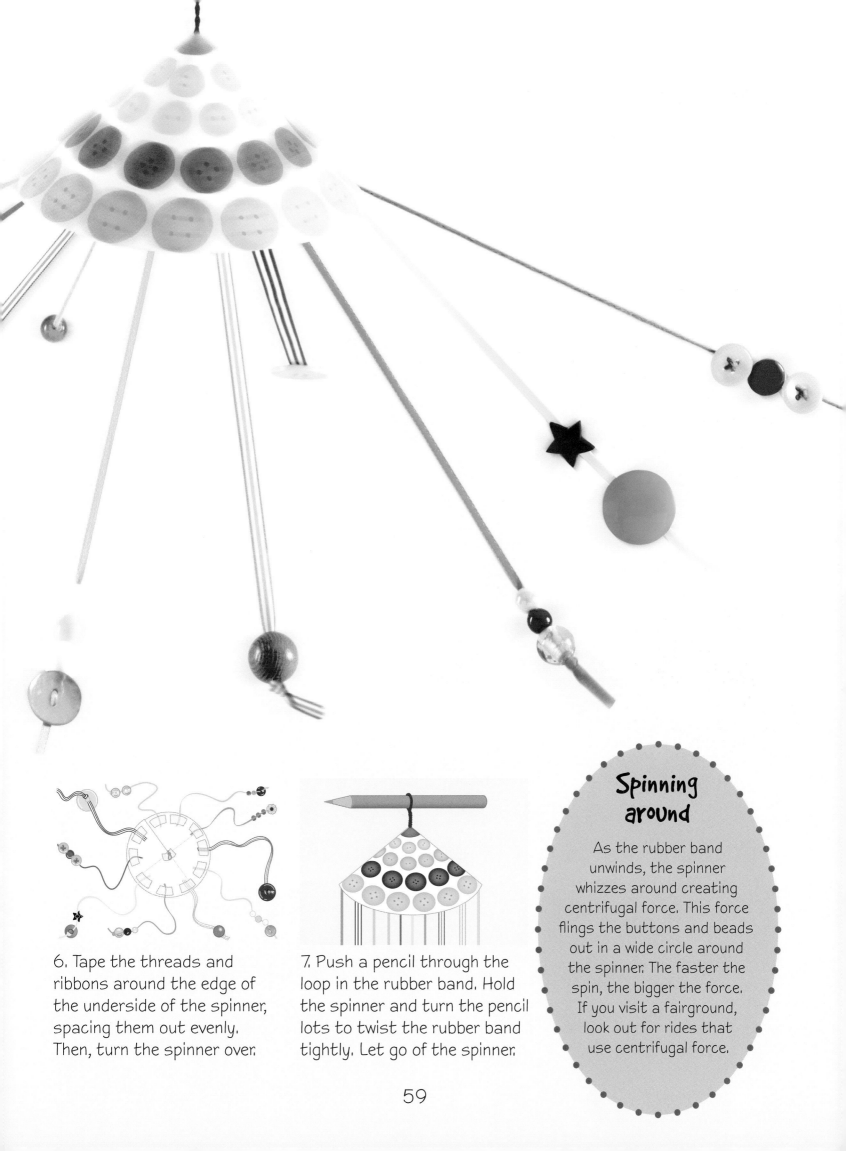

6. Tape the threads and ribbons around the edge of the underside of the spinner, spacing them out evenly. Then, turn the spinner over.

7. Push a pencil through the loop in the rubber band. Hold the spinner and turn the pencil lots to twist the rubber band tightly. Let go of the spinner.

Spinning around

As the rubber band unwinds, the spinner whizzes around creating centrifugal force. This force flings the buttons and beads out in a wide circle around the spinner. The faster the spin, the bigger the force. If you visit a fairground, look out for rides that use centrifugal force.

Magic monster heads

YOU WILL NEED: a balloon, a marker pen with permanent ink, a sweater

1. Blow up a balloon and knot the end. Draw a monster's face on one side of the balloon with a marker pen, then let the ink dry completely.

Don't rub the monster's face on your sweater.

2. Rub the balloon up and down on your sweater for a minute. Then, hold the balloon against a wall and let it go. It will stick to the wall.

Laws of attraction

When you rub a balloon on a sweater, a kind of energy called static electricity builds up on the balloon. When you hold the balloon near a wall, the static attracts it to the wall. The energy whizzes between the balloon and the wall, but when the energy weakens, the balloon drops down.

fishing game

YOU WILL NEED: felt-tip pens, tissue paper, a plastic ruler, a sweater

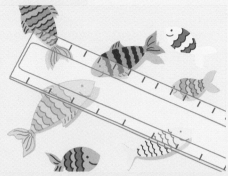

1. Using felt-tip pens, draw several little fish on different pieces of tissue paper. Then, cut them out and lay them on a flat surface.

2. Rub a plastic ruler on your sweater for about a minute. Then, hold it above the fish. Move it closer and closer to them, and see what happens.

Play with your friends and see who can pick up the most fish!

Catching a lift

The tissue paper fish lift up and stick onto the ruler because they're attracted to it by static electricity. Once you've rubbed the ruler on your sweater, it is charged up with static and can pick up the paper fish. Something like this can happen when you comb your hair, too — your comb can become statically charged then attract some of the hairs on your head.

fantastic flingers

YOU WILL NEED: thick paper, two drinking straws, corrugated cardboard, thread or string, poster tack, a clean lid from a plastic bottle

Crease the folds well.

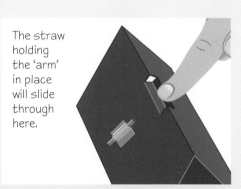

The straw holding the 'arm' in place will slide through here.

1. Cut a 30cm (12in) tall rectangle from thick paper. Fold one short edge about a third of the way down, then fold up the bottom edge.

2. Fold the paper into a triangular base and secure it with tape. Then, tape pieces of a straw onto the front and bottom of the base.

3. Make two small cuts in the top edge, about three finger widths apart. Then, push down the edge between the cuts, like this, to make a 'sleeve'.

Make sure the arm is narrower than the sleeve.

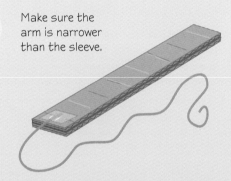

The front part of the arm should be shorter than the back.

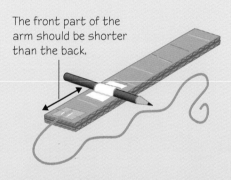

Slide the straw through the curved paper strip.

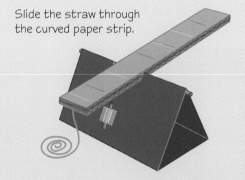

4. Cut two 30cm (12in) strips from corrugated cardboard and glue them together for an 'arm'. Tape a long thread onto the front end of the arm.

5. Cut a small strip of paper. Lay a pencil across the arm, then lay the paper strip on top and glue the ends onto the arm. Slide the pencil out.

6. Turn the arm over and lay the curved paper strip in the sleeve. Slide a straw through from one side of the base to the other, like this.

Put one blob on each corner of the base.

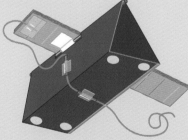

7. Push the thread through the straw on the front, then through the straw on the bottom. Press big blobs of poster tack on for feet.

8. Glue a clean lid onto the long end of the arm. Press the flinger onto a surface and put a toy in the lid. Tug the string to send the toy flying!

Ready to launch

The arm of the flinger works like a lever. By tugging on the thread, you suddenly force one end of the arm to swing down. As it goes down, the other end is forced up into the air. This action launches the toy sitting on the end of the arm. The energy you used to tug the thread is transferred into the arm and used to fling the toy.

These flingers were wrapped in paper in step 4 before the thread was taped on.

Tricks of the eye

Invisible shapes

YOU WILL NEED: thick paper, poster tack, a coin, a felt-tip pen

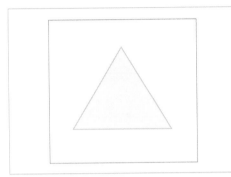

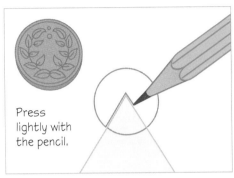

Press lightly with the pencil.

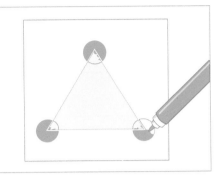

1. Cut a triangle from thick paper. Press a blob of poster tack onto the back of it, then press the triangle onto a piece of paper.

2. Lay a coin over one of the points of the triangle. Draw around the coin, then move it off. Draw around the point of the triangle inside the circle.

3. Draw circles on the other two points. Fill in the shapes around the points with a felt-tip pen, then remove the triangle. What do you see?

Seeing things...

The first thing that you see when you look at the picture is a triangle that isn't there. This is because your brain takes clues from what you see and fills in the blanks. Even though all you can see are three shapes with a 'V' taken out of them, the way that they are arranged makes your brain 'see' a missing triangle.

This trick works with wonky triangles, too.

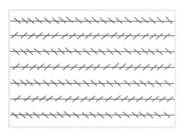

Wonky lines?

YOU WILL NEED: lined paper, a pencil or pen

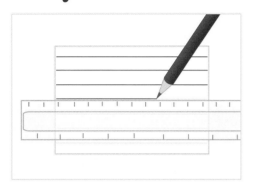

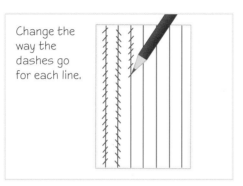

Change the way the dashes go for each line.

If they don't think the lines are parallel, show them the back of the paper.

1. Cut a piece of lined paper, then draw over the lines using a ruler. Then, turn the paper around so that the lines are vertical (going up and down).

2. Draw short diagonal dashes down the first line, then draw dashes going the other way down the next line. Draw dashes on all the lines.

3. Turn the paper again so that the lines are horizontal (going across). Ask someone if they think the lines are parallel (evenly spaced and straight).

Tricky flowers

YOU WILL NEED: paper, a medium-sized coin, a pen lid, a big coin, felt-tip pens

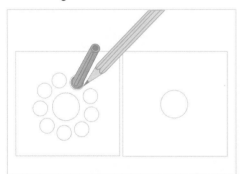

Use a different shade for the petals.

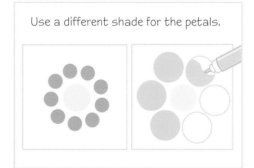

3. Ask someone to pick the flower with the biggest middle. Then, lay the medium-sized coin over each middle to show they are both the same size.

1. Use a pencil to draw around a medium-sized coin in the middle of two pieces of paper. Draw around a pen lid to make small petals around one circle.

2. Draw around a big coin to add big petals to the other circle. Then, fill in the flowers, making both middles the same shade of yellow.

optical illusion

In both experiments, your brain is tricked into thinking something is different from how it really is. When you look at the lines, the dashes mean that your brain cannot see the straight lines clearly. The dashes are all at different angles, so it assumes that the parallel lines are too.

With the flowers, the small petals make the middle circle seem big compared to them, but the big petals make it look small.

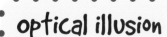

Squirty whale

YOU WILL NEED: thick paper, pencils, a drinking straw, a rounded balloon

Keep the fold at the top of the paper.

  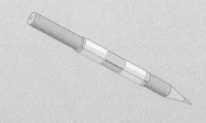

1. Fold a big piece of thick paper in half. Draw a whale's body with its top against the fold. Add a tail, then add a half-circle for a blowhole.

2. Use pencils to decorate the whale's tummy, then draw eyes and a mouth. Keeping the paper folded, cut out the whale and the blowhole.

3. Cut a rectangle from thick paper, making it about half the height of the whale. Roll the paper around a pencil, then tape it to make a tube.

Water pressure

When you pour water into the balloon, the water completely fills the space inside. By squeezing the balloon, you're suddenly making that space smaller. The water that was inside is forced out at high pressure. It whooshes up the straw and a jet of water shoots out.

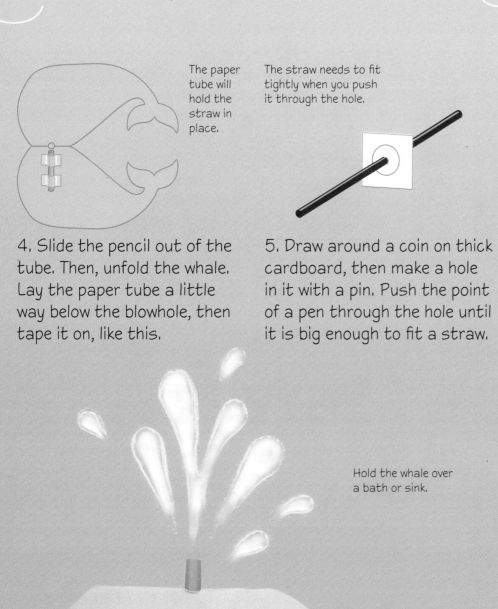

The paper tube will hold the straw in place.

The straw needs to fit tightly when you push it through the hole.

Cut a piece off the end of the straw to make it a little shorter.

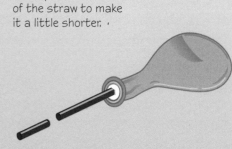

4. Slide the pencil out of the tube. Then, unfold the whale. Lay the paper tube a little way below the blowhole, then tape it on, like this.

5. Draw around a coin on thick cardboard, then make a hole in it with a pin. Push the point of a pen through the hole until it is big enough to fit a straw.

6. Cut out the circle and push the straw through the hole again. Then, slide the straw into a balloon and stretch the neck over the cardboard circle.

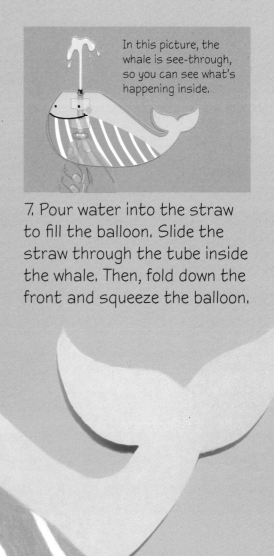

In this picture, the whale is see-through, so you can see what's happening inside.

Hold the whale over a bath or sink.

7. Pour water into the straw to fill the balloon. Slide the straw through the tube inside the whale. Then, fold down the front and squeeze the balloon.

City skyline

YOU WILL NEED: thin dark cardboard and chalk

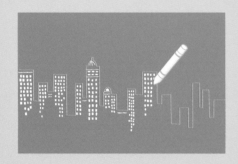

1. Draw a city skyline across the middle of a piece of thin dark cardboard. Add dots of white chalk for windows. Then, cut along the skyline.

2. Try standing the skyline up. It won't stand up on its own, so fold it in half. Fold the ends in to meet the fold, like this. Now try standing it up again.

Balancing act

At first, the skyline can't support itself, because its centre of gravity is unable to stay over its base. If the paper leans at all, this point moves away from the base and the skyline falls over.

centre of gravity

Folding the skyline makes it much more stable. It now has to lean over a lot before its centre of gravity moves outside its base.

centre of gravity

Triangle tower

YOU WILL NEED: thin cardboard

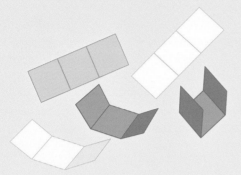

1. Cut five cardboard strips that are 12cm (6in) long. Make marks 4cm (2in) and 8cm (4in) along each strip, then make folds at the marks.

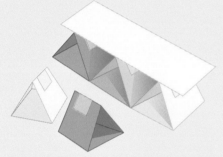

2. Tape the strips into triangles, like this. Put three triangles in a line next to each other. Then, cut a strip of cardboard and lay it on top.

Put an object in the middle, then add more.

3. Stand two triangles on top, then cut a shorter strip and lay it on top of the two triangles. Try putting different objects on top of the tower.

The tower looks quite flimsy, but it can hold a bigger weight than you might think.

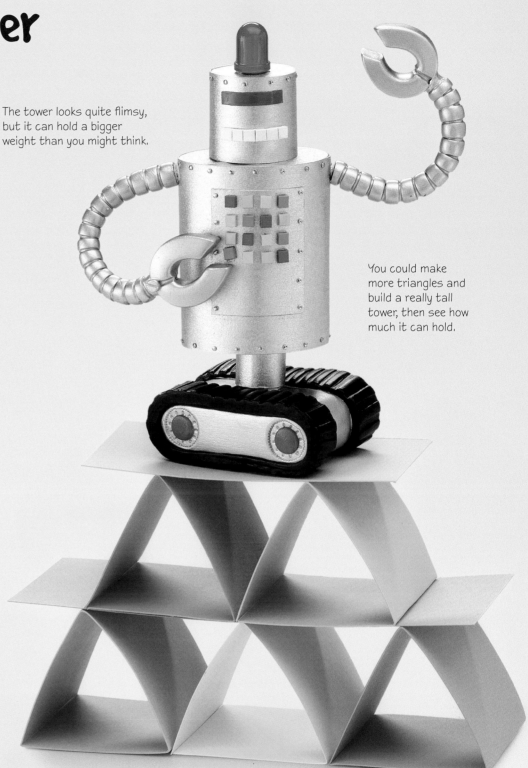

You could make more triangles and build a really tall tower, then see how much it can hold.

Strong support

The tower can support a large weight because it is made of triangles — the strongest shapes of all. Triangles are strong because they have a small point at the top and a wide base.

The weight above presses down on the point of the triangle...

...spreads evenly down the sides...

...and out over the base.

Tasty bread rolls

YOU WILL NEED: 450g strong white bread flour, 1 teaspoon salt, 2 teaspoons dried easy-blend yeast, 300ml warm water that has been boiled, 2 tablespoons vegetable oil, milk, a greased baking tray

1. Sift the flour and salt through a sieve into a large bowl. Add the yeast and stir it in, then make a hollow in the middle of the flour.

2. Pour the warm water into a jug and add the oil, then pour the mixture into the hollow. Stir everything with a wooden spoon to make a soft dough.

You could sprinkle poppy or sesame seeds, rolled oats or a little grated cheese over the tops of the rolls before you put them in the oven.

These brown rolls were made with wholemeal bread flour instead of white flour.

Hungry fungi

Yeast doesn't look very lively, but it's actually alive. It's made up of teeny tiny living things called micro-organisms. Yeast feeds off a chemical in the flour called starch. As it does this, it gives off a gas that gets trapped in the dough, making it rise. When you break open a bread roll, you can see where the bubbles of gas were trapped inside.

Knead the dough firmly.

3. Dust a clean work surface with flour. Put the dough onto the work surface. To knead the dough, press your knuckles into it. Push it away from you.

The dough will feel soft and springy.

4. Fold the dough in half and turn it around. Push it away from you again, then fold it in half and turn it around. Knead the dough for 10 minutes.

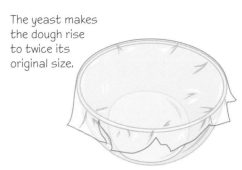
The yeast makes the dough rise to twice its original size.

5. Put the dough into a clean bowl and cover the bowl with plastic foodwrap. Then, leave the bowl in a warm place for 1½ hours to rise.

6. Sprinkle more flour onto the work surface, then put the dough onto it. Knead the dough again for a minute, to squeeze out any bubbles.

7. Break the dough into 12 pieces. Roll the pieces into balls and put them onto a greased baking tray with spaces between them.

8. Leave the rolls to rise in a warm place for about 40 minutes. While they are rising, heat your oven to 220°C, 425°F, gas mark 7.

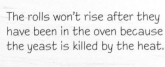
The rolls won't rise after they have been in the oven because the yeast is killed by the heat.

9. Brush a little milk over the tops of the rolls. Then, make crosses in the top of some of them by carefully cutting into the dough with a sharp knife.

Wear oven mitts.

10. Bake the rolls for 12-15 minutes. Wearing oven mitts, lift the tray out of the oven. After two minutes, move the rolls onto a wire rack to cool.

Salty dragon painting

YOU WILL NEED: thick white paper, very watery paint, salt (big crystals work best), black paper

Use a pencil.

1. Draw an oval for a dragon's body on thick white paper. Draw a head with a snout, then join the head and body with a curving neck.

2. Draw a long pointed tail and add a triangle on the end. Then, draw a fanned-out wing coming out from the dragon's back, like this.

3. Draw two legs with claws, coming out from the dragon's tummy. Then, add spikes on the back of the head and along the neck.

Make a dragon breathe fire by drawing flames with chalk, then rubbing them with your fingertip.

Sucking salt

Salt crystals 'suck up' or absorb water. When you sprinkle salt onto watery paint, each crystal absorbs some of the paint from around it. This means that there is more paint around the salt crystals than on the rest of the paper. When you brush off the salt, you can see darker patches of paint where the crystals lay on the paper.

You could glue on a landscape cut from a big piece of painted paper that has been sprinkled with salt.

4. Brush lots of watery paint all over the dragon, but don't worry if you go over the outlines. Sprinkle lots of salt crystals over the wet paint.

5. Leave the paint to dry, then brush off the salt. Then, use a thin black pen to draw an eye, a mouth, and a nostril. Draw over the lines on the wing, too.

6. Using the pencil lines as a guide, cut around the dragon. Then, spread glue on the back of the dragon and press it onto a piece of black paper.

Singing bottles

YOU WILL NEED: several clean glass bottles, including three that are the same size, and water

1. Half-fill three equal-sized glass bottles with cold water. Then, pour half of the water from one bottle into one of the others.

Blow here

(You may need to move your head up or down to hear a noise.)

2. Move your head so that your lower lip is close to the top of one bottle. Blow across the bottle until you hear a singing sound.

Lowest   Highest

3. Blow across the other two bottles, listening to the sounds they make. Then, arrange the bottles in order of the notes they make.

Adding a few drops of food dye makes it easier to see how much is in each bottle.

4. Pour water into lots more bottles. Blow across them, then pour water into and out of them, to make as many different notes as you can.

Try blowing a tune using the singing bottles.

Singing sounds

Blowing across the top of a bottle makes the air inside vibrate. This moving air makes a musical note. The note you hear depends on how much air there is inside the bottle. By filling part of the bottle with water, you change how much air is inside. When there's lots of water and less air, you will hear a higher note.

Panpipe straws

YOU WILL NEED: eight drinking straws and cardboard

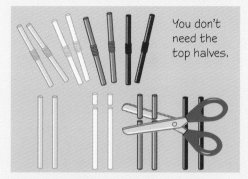

You don't need the top halves.

1. Cut eight drinking straws in half. Cut a short piece off two of the half straws. Then, cut a slightly longer piece off two of the others.

2. Cut an even longer piece off two of the remaining half straws. Then, lay the straws in a line in size order. They will now be four different lengths.

Line up the ends of the straws with the edge of the sticky tape.

3. Cut a long piece of sticky tape and lay it sticky-side up. Press the straws onto it, in size order, then press the ends of the tape over the straws.

You could decorate your panpipes with stickers from the middle of this book.

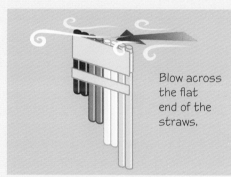

Blow across the flat end of the straws.

4. Cut two cardboard strips the width of the straws. Glue them onto the straws. Then, blow across the ends of the straws to make a sound.

Each pair of straws makes a different note, so you can make more notes by using more straws.

Whistling wind

When you blow across the ends of the straws, it makes the air inside them vibrate, and they make different sounds. Long straws make deeper sounds than short ones. Many instruments, including panpipes, flutes and recorders, make sounds using vibrations.

Ink spots and stripes

YOU WILL NEED: coffee filter papers, felt-tip pens, narrow glasses, water

Spots

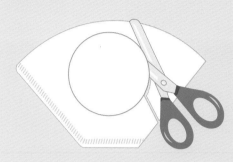

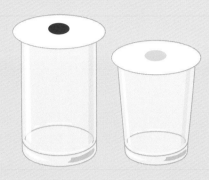

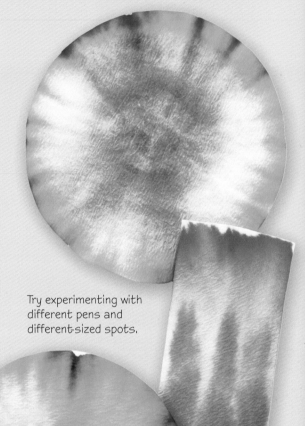

1. Lay a mug on a coffee filter paper and draw around it with a pencil. Then, holding both layers of the filter paper together, cut out the circle.

2. Using two different felt-tip pens, draw a large spot in the middle of each circle of paper. Then, lay each one on the top of a narrow glass, like this.

Try experimenting with different pens and different-sized spots.

The ink will start to spread out.

3. Using your finger, drip a drop of water onto each ink spot. Then, drip a few more drops onto each one and leave the paper circles to dry.

You'll find that some inks are made up from more pigments than others.

Stripes

1. Cut some narrow strips from a coffee filter paper. Then, using felt-tip pens, draw a line of large spots near the bottom of each strip.

The spots need to be at the bottom.

2. Pour a little water into a glass. Dip each paper strip into the water for a minute, then lift it out. Tape each one onto a pencil to dry, like this.

Spreading out

Although you can't tell when you look at them, inks are made up of different pigments. For example, orange ink could be a mixture of yellow and red pigments. When water touches an ink spot, the ink dissolves into it, spreads out and separates into the pigments that make it up. This doesn't happen with 'permanent' inks, because they don't dissolve in water.

77

You could paint stripes or spots on your bug before you glue on the eyes, wings and feelers.

Bouncing bugs

YOU WILL NEED: kitchen foil, sewing elastic or a long rubber band, tissue paper, thick paper

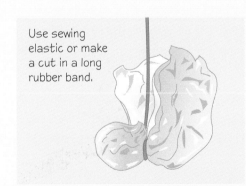

Use sewing elastic or make a cut in a long rubber band.

1. Cut a foil square for a bug's body. Scrunch it in the middle, then tie a long piece of elastic around the scrunched part. Squeeze the foil into a ball.

Pull the elastic out to one side.

2. Rip lots of small pieces from tissue paper. Lay the bug on a piece of plastic foodwrap, then brush part of the bug with white glue.

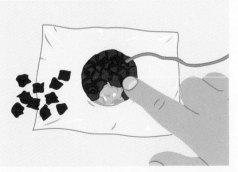

3. Press pieces of tissue paper onto the glue. Brush on more glue and press on more paper until the bug is covered, then leave it to dry.

fantastic elastic

The elastic stretches and becomes really long and thin when you pull the bug down. When you let go, it pings back up again and returns to its original shape. This is called elasticity. Not many things are elastic. Lots of things don't change shape at all, no matter how hard you try to change them. Other things can stretch and stretch, but when you let go, they stay that way and don't ping back to their original shape.

You could use stickers from the middle of this book to decorate your bug.

Don't cut here.

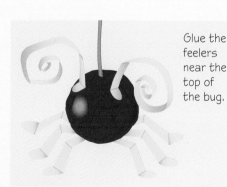

Glue the feelers near the top of the bug.

4. Fold a piece of thick paper in half. Draw a rectangle along the fold, then add three legs. Keeping the paper folded, cut out the shape and open it out.

5. Glue the legs onto the body, then bend them a little. Cut two paper feelers and use your fingers to curl them. Bend the ends over, then glue them on.

6. Cut and glue on foil wings. Press on eyes and draw a mouth. Tie the elastic to the back of a chair, pull the bug down, then release it.

Monster in the city drawing

YOU WILL NEED: paper, a ruler, pencils

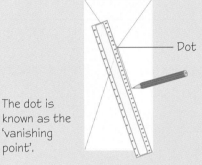

— Dot

The dot is known as the 'vanishing point'.

1. Draw a dot halfway across a piece of paper, part of the way down. Use a ruler to draw lines from the dot to the corners of the paper.

2. Draw vertical lines for buildings between the diagonal lines. Draw them further apart at the edges, getting closer nearer the vanishing point.

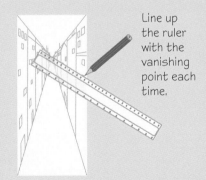

Line up the ruler with the vanishing point each time.

3. Draw roofs on top of some of the buildings. Then, add some doors and windows, using the ruler to draw their top edges, like this.

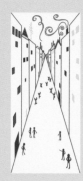

Make the people in the distance smaller than the ones in the foreground.

4. Go over the outlines and fill in the doors and windows with bright pencils. Add people on the road, then erase any pencil lines.

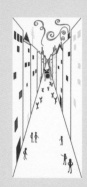

See what happens to the size of the monster in relation to the people and buildings as you move it.

5. Draw a small monster on another piece of paper. Cut it out and put it on the far end of the road. Then, move it 'nearer' to you, down the road.

Big and small

Drawing a city in this way makes the picture look 3-dimensional. Buildings that are far away look smaller than ones nearby. This is called perspective, and your brain uses this to judge how near or far things are from you. The monster will seem big when it's 'far away' and tiny when you move it nearer!

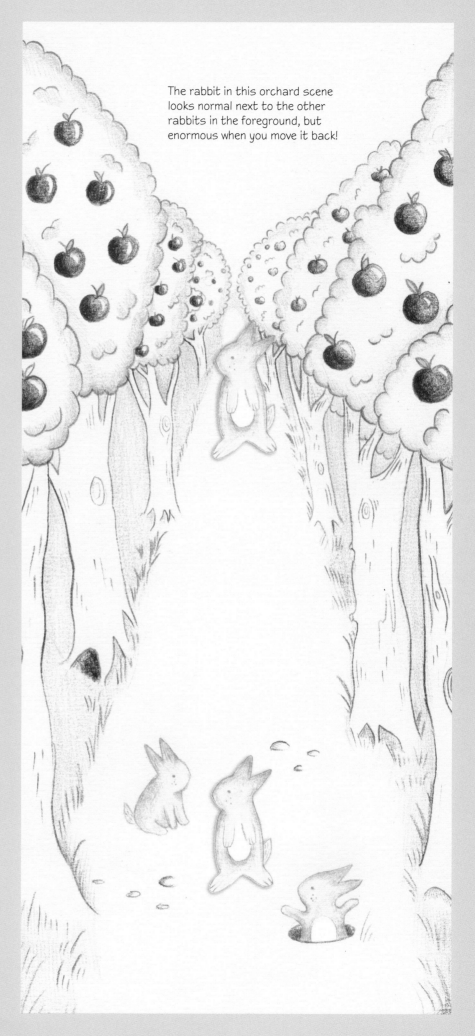

The rabbit in this orchard scene looks normal next to the other rabbits in the foreground, but enormous when you move it back!

Spinning paper helicopter

YOU WILL NEED: paper and a paperclip

1. Cut a strip of paper that is 5 x 20cm (2 x 8in) in size. Draw a line down the middle with a pencil. Then, fold down the top third of the paper.

2. Unfold the paper. To make helicopter 'blades', cut down the line, as far as the fold. Draw a line across the paper, a little way below the fold.

3. Make marks on the line you have drawn, halfway between each edge and the middle. Then, cut in from each edge, up to the mark.

82

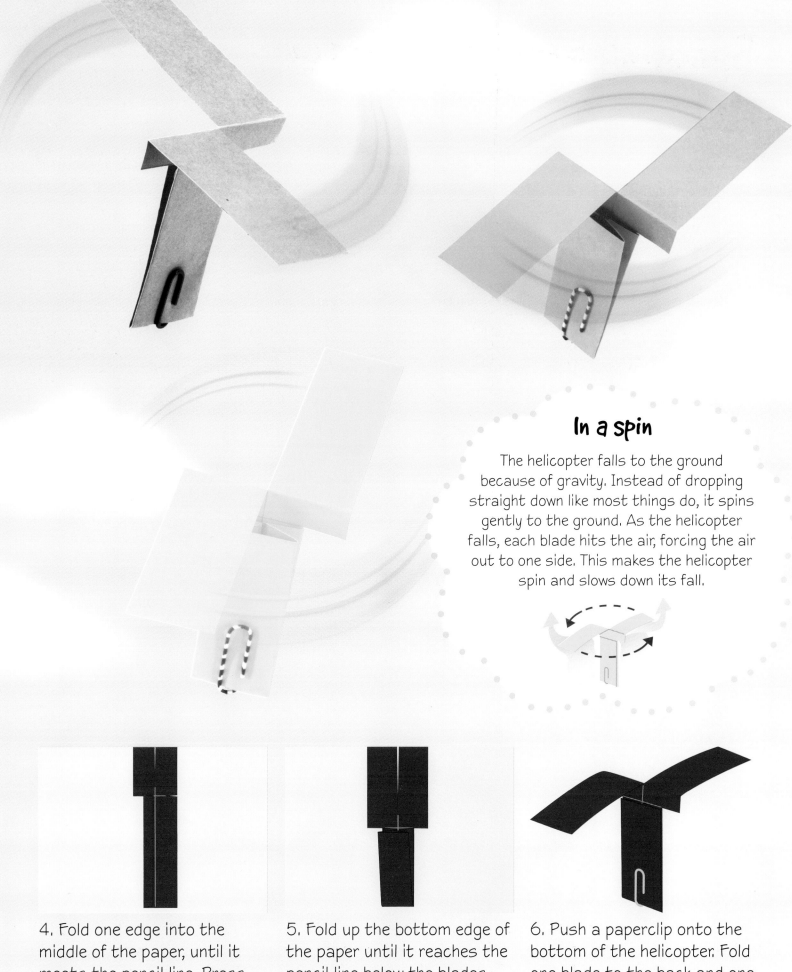

In a spin

The helicopter falls to the ground because of gravity. Instead of dropping straight down like most things do, it spins gently to the ground. As the helicopter falls, each blade hits the air, forcing the air out to one side. This makes the helicopter spin and slows down its fall.

4. Fold one edge into the middle of the paper, until it meets the pencil line. Press the fold down well, then fold over the other edge, too.

5. Fold up the bottom edge of the paper until it reaches the pencil line below the blades. Crease the fold well, so that the paper lies flat.

6. Push a paperclip onto the bottom of the helicopter. Fold one blade to the back and one to the front. Then, throw the helicopter high into the air.

83

Bendy balancers

YOU WILL NEED: pipe cleaners, a long piece of thread, two chairs, beads that you can thread onto pipe cleaners

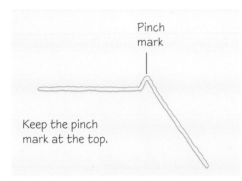

Pinch mark

Keep the pinch mark at the top.

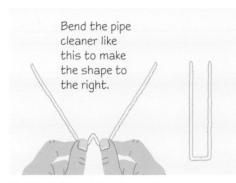

Bend the pipe cleaner like this to make the shape to the right.

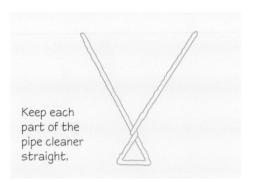

Keep each part of the pipe cleaner straight.

1. Bend a pipe cleaner in half, and pinch the middle. Bend one side out, a finger width from the pinch mark. Then, bend the other side up, too.

2. Holding the two bends that you've just made, carefully flatten the pinch mark to make a squared-off 'U' shape, like this.

3. Bend both sides of the pipe cleaner into the middle, until they cross over. Then twist them over each other, to keep them in place.

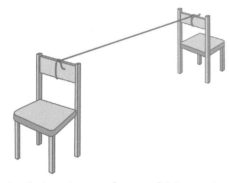

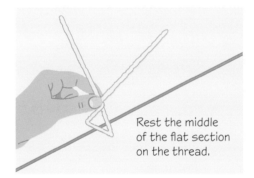

Rest the middle of the flat section on the thread.

4. Cut a long piece of thread. Tie each end of the thread to the back of a chair. Move the chairs apart until the thread is tightly stretched out.

5. Keeping the flat middle section at the bottom, try to balance the pipe cleaner on the thread. Can you get the pipe cleaner to balance?

You can find out more about how things balance on pages 38-39 and page 68.

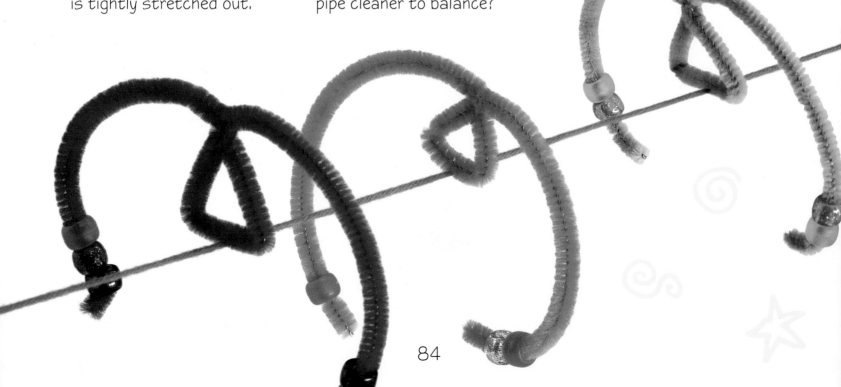

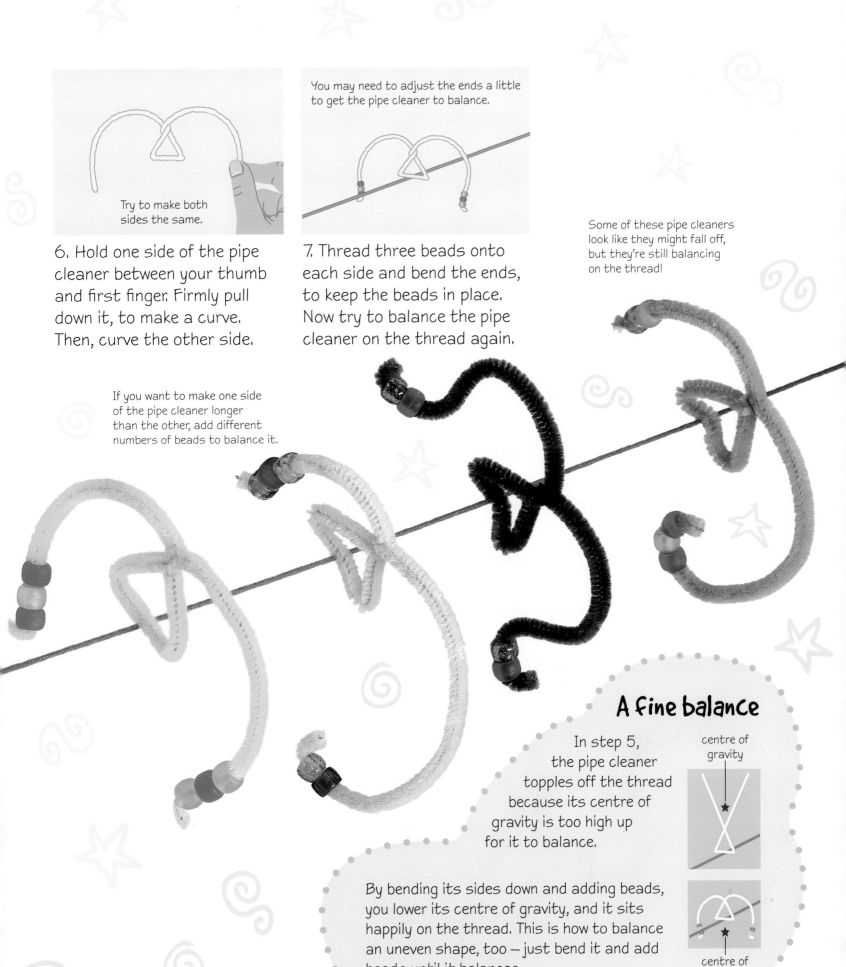

Try to make both
sides the same.

6. Hold one side of the pipe
cleaner between your thumb
and first finger. Firmly pull
down it, to make a curve.
Then, curve the other side.

You may need to adjust the ends a little
to get the pipe cleaner to balance.

7. Thread three beads onto
each side and bend the ends,
to keep the beads in place.
Now try to balance the pipe
cleaner on the thread again.

Some of these pipe cleaners
look like they might fall off,
but they're still balancing
on the thread!

If you want to make one side
of the pipe cleaner longer
than the other, add different
numbers of beads to balance it.

A fine balance

In step 5,
the pipe cleaner
topples off the thread
because its centre of
gravity is too high up
for it to balance.

centre of
gravity

By bending its sides down and adding beads,
you lower its centre of gravity, and it sits
happily on the thread. This is how to balance
an uneven shape, too — just bend it and add
beads until it balances.

centre of
gravity

Light catcher

YOU WILL NEED: white paper, clear plastic from a large sandwich bag, cellophane or see-through chocolate wrappers, tissue paper, plain thick papers, poster tack

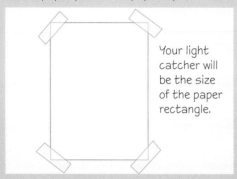

Your light catcher will be the size of the paper rectangle.

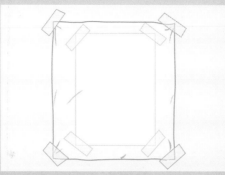

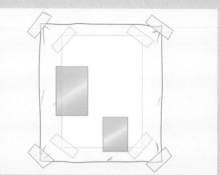

1. Cut a rectangle from white paper. Lay the rectangle on a work surface, then press a piece of sticky tape over each corner to keep it in place.

2. Cut a rectangle of clear plastic that is bigger than the white rectangle. Lay the plastic over the rectangle, then tape down the corners.

3. Cut two or more shapes from cellophane and glue them onto the plastic. Glue them on so that they overlap the edges of the white rectangle.

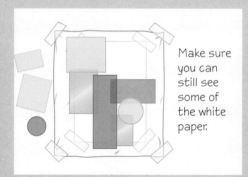

Make sure you can still see some of the white paper.

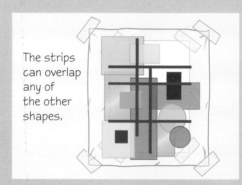

The strips can overlap any of the other shapes.

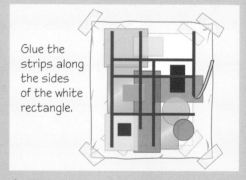

Glue the strips along the sides of the white rectangle.

4. Cut some more shapes from tissue paper. Then, glue them onto the plastic so that they overlap the cellophane shapes a little.

5. Cut some small shapes from plain paper and glue them onto the light catcher. Then, cut a few thin strips of paper and glue them on, too.

6. To make a frame, cut two paper strips that are a little longer than the white rectangle. Glue the strips onto the plastic.

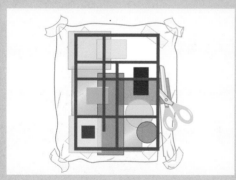

Passing through

You can see right through the plastic and cellophane, because they are completely see-through, or transparent. Tissue paper is translucent, which means that it lets some light through, but not much. The plain paper is opaque – no light gets through it at all.

7. Cut two strips that will fit along the top and bottom of the rectangle and glue them on. When the glue is dry, trim the plastic around the frame.

8. Turn the light catcher over and press poster tack onto the corners. Then, press it onto a window so that light shines through it.

floating water beastie

YOU WILL NEED: thin cardboard, pencils, a large container or sink

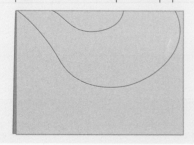
Keep the fold at the top of the paper.

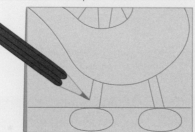
Make the spikes touch the fold.

1. Fold a rectangle of thin cardboard in half, so that its short ends are together. Draw a shape for a beastie's body, with a curve for its back.

2. Add spikes along the back. Then, draw a line across the paper, a little way above the bottom. Draw two big feet below it, then add two legs.

3. Holding the layers together, cut around the shape, taking care not to cut along the fold. Then, decorate the beastie with pencils.

You could make a beastie with six legs.

Lower the beastie onto the water so that all four feet touch the water at the same time.

4. To make the beastie stand, fold out its feet until they lie flat. Fill a large container with water and carefully place the beastie on top of the water.

Big feet

The surface of water is like a very thin skin. The beastie's big feet spread its weight over the top of this 'skin', and it floats. If it had very small feet, they would break through the water's skin and the beastie would sink.

Soap-powered fish

YOU WILL NEED: thin cardboard, wax crayons, a large clean dish, a toothpick or satay stick, liquid soap or washing-up liquid

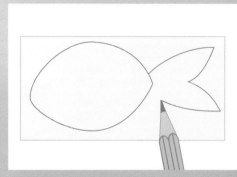

1. Draw a fish's body on thin cardboard. Add a pointed tail, then cut out the fish. Use wax crayons to decorate the fish, then add a face with black pen.

2. Fill a large dish with water. Then, use a toothpick or satay stick to dab a blob of liquid soap or washing-up liquid around the 'V' in the fish's tail.

3. Hold the fish flat above the water, with its tail near the edge of the dish. Carefully lay the fish on the water, then watch to see what it does.

If you want to do this project more than once, thoroughly rinse and dry your dish each time or your fish won't move.

Super soap

The skin on the surface of the water is held together by a force called surface tension. When the soap on the fish's tail touches the water, it forms a soapy film behind the fish that pushes the skin on the water away. This propels the fish forward in the water.

catapult plane

YOU WILL NEED: paper, a rubber band, a pencil

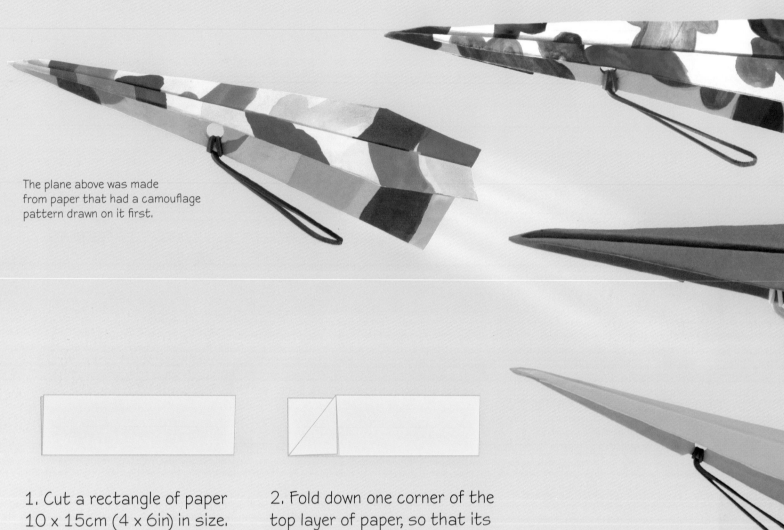

The plane above was made from paper that had a camouflage pattern drawn on it first.

1. Cut a rectangle of paper 10 x 15cm (4 x 6in) in size. Fold the rectangle in half so that the long sides are together. Crease the fold well.

2. Fold down one corner of the top layer of paper, so that its edge lines up with the bottom fold. Turn the paper over and fold down the other corner, too.

3. Fold down the corner of the top layer again, so that the folds line up at the bottom. Use a small piece of sticky tape to hold it in place.

4. Turn the plane over. Fold down the other corner in the same way and tape it. Then, fold down the long edge to make one of the plane's wings.

Fold it so that the long folded edge meets the bottom edge.

5. Turn the paper over and fold down the other wing in the same way. Then, fold both of the wings back up again, and lay the plane flat.

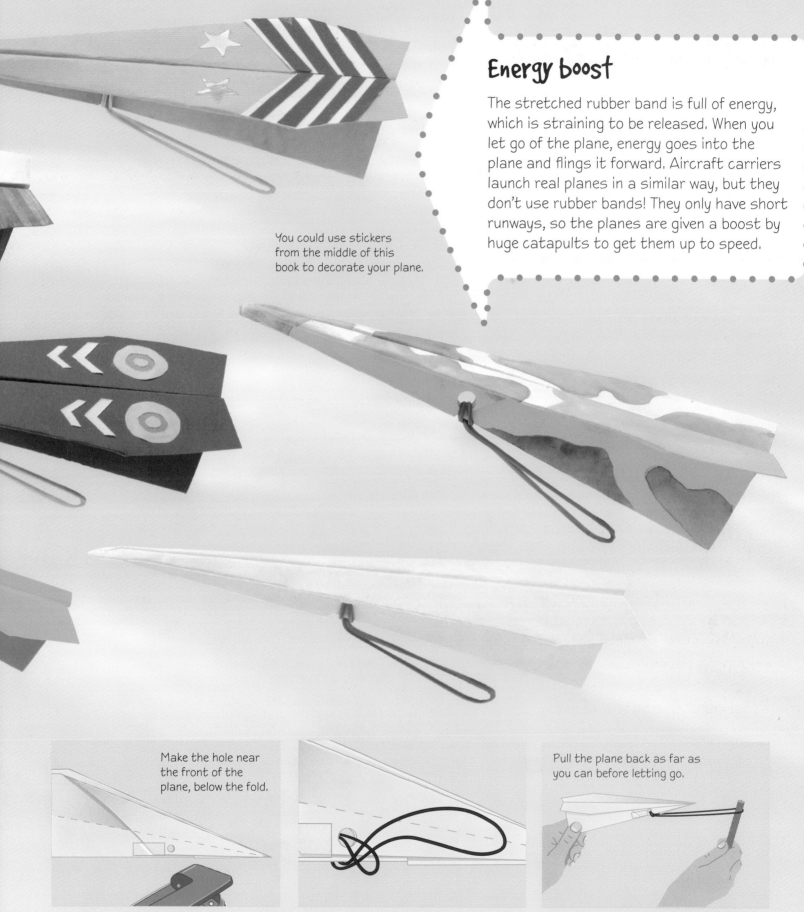

Energy boost

The stretched rubber band is full of energy, which is straining to be released. When you let go of the plane, energy goes into the plane and flings it forward. Aircraft carriers launch real planes in a similar way, but they don't use rubber bands! They only have short runways, so the planes are given a boost by huge catapults to get them up to speed.

You could use stickers from the middle of this book to decorate your plane.

Make the hole near the front of the plane, below the fold.

Pull the plane back as far as you can before letting go.

6. Use one side of a hole punch to make a hole part way along the plane. Test making holes in a scrap of paper, so you know how to position the hole punch.

7. Thread one end of a rubber band through the hole in the plane. Bend the other end around and push it through the loop, like this. Pull it tight.

8. Fold the wings down so that they stick out. Then, loop the rubber band over the top of a pencil or pen. Pull the plane back, then let it go.

Blow-painted monster

YOU WILL NEED: paints, water, thick paper, a drinking straw

Nothing much will happen when you blow at the paint.

The two paints will start to merge.

1. Mix some paint with water in a clean yogurt pot, to make the paint runny. Then, mix another shade of runny paint in another yogurt pot.

2. Pour some of one paint onto a piece of thick paper. Pour some of the other paint next to it. Then, try blowing hard at the paint.

3. Now hold a straw above the paint. Blow hard, to make the paint spread out in different directions. Keep blowing until you make a monster shape.

You can decorate your monster with anything you like – spots, hairs or even wings.

4. Use the end of the straw to drag loops for eyes, and little lines for legs and arms. When the paint is dry, draw eyes and a mouth on your monster.

A blast of air

When you blow air normally, it spreads out and loses pressure when it leaves your mouth. It's hard to aim it in any particular direction. But when you blow air through a straw, it's forced through a narrow gap, which makes a high-pressure jet that you can direct at the paint.

Oozing slime

YOU WILL NEED: cornflour, water, food dye

1. Half-fill a small glass with cornflour, then tip it into a large bowl. Add quarter of a glass of cold water, and a few drops of food dye, too.

It takes a few minutes to mix it all together.

2. Start to stir everything together using a metal spoon. Then, mix it with your hands until everything is completely mixed.

3. Punch the slime in the bowl, to see how it feels. Then, roll some of it into a ball. Hold the ball in one of your hands and see what happens.

Solid or liquid?

As you'll have discovered, the slime feels solid when you punch it, but runny when you hold it. Most things are solid, liquid or gas, but the slime is like a solid AND a liquid. The slime is made up from tiny little things called particles. When it's a liquid, they are spread out, and the slime is gloopy and runs through your fingers. When you punch it, you squash the particles together and it feels like a solid.

93

Websites to visit

On the Usborne Quicklinks Website, there are links to 50 fantastic websites where you can find out more about science, do activities online, and discover more experiments to do. To visit these websites, go to www.usborne-quicklinks.com read the internet safety guidelines, then type in the keywords "science things".

Fascinating things to find out

Website 1: Read about scientists who made history.

Website 2: Look at lots of amazing tessellations created by an artist named Escher.

Website 3: Discover what's under your skin.

Website 4: Find out about Einstein — one of the world's most famous scientists.

Website 5: See some weird inventions.

Website 6: Discover how artists use perspective.

Website 7: Find out about surface tension.

Website 8: Watch some animations about solids, liquids and gases.

Website 9: Why do magazines use dotted pictures?

Website 10: Learn more about gravity and space.

Website 11: Answers to some questions about science in everyday life.

Website 12: A site that gives information about what's happening now in the world of science.

Website 13: How does static cause lightning?

This triangle tower is on page 69.

More science things to do

Website 14: Try some experiments with water and find out what's happening.

Website 15: Experiment with your senses.

Website 16: Find out how to make 3-D shapes.

Website 17: Investigate pigment in a jelly bean.

Website 18: Discover what amazing things you can do with air.

Website 19: Some simple experiments with things from around the home.

Website 20: Make your own paper.

Website 21: Try some optical illusion experiments, then find out how they work.

Website 22: Send a secret mirror message.

Website 23: Make animal hand shadows.

Website 24: Find out how to walk through a piece of paper.

Website 25: Things to grow and eat.

Website 26: Lots more science experiments to try.

Experiment online

Website 27: Use a pivot to lift a hippo.

Website 28: Grow a plant online.

Website 29: Play with shadows.

Website 30: Experiment with paints and pigments.

Website 31: Test your senses in a timed quiz.

Website 32: See what happens when you bend
and stretch different materials.

Website 33: Design a car and take it for a test drive.

Website 34: Test friction in different materials.

Website 35: Experiments to try online or at home.

online games and activities

Website 36: A game about lines of symmetry.

Website 37: Zoom through a 3-D world of science.

Website 38: Use toys to make a kaleidoscope.

Website 39: Reflect shapes in this fun game.

Website 40: Try some tessellations.

Website 41: Look at optical illusions that will baffle your eyes and your brain.

Website 42: Explore science in the world around you.

Website 43: Figure out how energy can be turned from one form into another.

Website 44: Find out more about levers and other simple machines.

Website 45: Take a mirror challenge and see if you can reflect light onto different objects.

Website 46: A great site packed with things to read, quizzes and games all about science.

Website 47: Learn facts about sound whilst completing an underwater mission.

Website 48: Ride on a rollercoaster and use your science knowledge to get to the end.

Website 49: Make an online kaleidoscope and learn more about symmetry.

Website 50: Take a challenge to test your knowledge about the science of light.

Instructions for
these dangly monkeys
are on pages 28-29.

Some of these websites require "plug-ins" — programs that your web browser needs in order to play videos, animations and sounds. You probably have these already, but if not, you can download them free from the Net Help area of the Usborne Quicklinks Website.

The links in Usborne Quickinks are regularly reviewed and updated, but websites occasionally close down and when this happens, we replace them. When you visit Usborne Quicklinks, the links may be slightly different from those described in the book. Usborne Publishing is not responsible, and does not accept liability, for the content or availability of any website other than its own. We recommend that children are supervised while on the internet.

Index

absorbing, 23, 55, 73
air, 9, 23, 83
    moving, 44-45, 48
    pressure, 24, 49, 92
    vibrations, 74, 75
asymmetry, 33

balance, 28-29, 39, 68,
    84-85
beans, 22-23
bicarbonate of soda, 7, 16,
    17
bleaching, 46-47

carbon dioxide, 18
centrifugal force, 58-59
chemicals, 47, 70
chemical reaction, 7, 17

density, 19, 43
dilution, 52-53
dissolving, 43, 77

elasticity, 78-79
electricity, static, 60, 61
energy, 23, 60, 63, 91
    wind, 13
eyes, 25, 36, 37, 64, 65

fingerprints, 10-11
floating, 18, 19, 24, 43, 88
force, 29
    centrifugal, 58-59
    friction, 56-57

surface tension, 88, 89
freezing, 42, 43
friction, 56-57

gas, 7, 18, 70, 93
germination, 23
gravity, 39, 68, 83, 85

ink, 52, 53, 54, 76, 77
    invisible, 16-17

kaleidoscope, 41

leaves, 23, 34-35, 54
levers, 62-63
light, 23, 86
    reflecting , 21, 40, 41
    shadows, 15
liquid, 18, 19, 31, 42,
    53, 93

melting, 30-31, 42, 43
micro-organisms, 70

opaque, 86
optical illusions, 64-65

particles, 31, 53, 93
perspective, 80-81
petals, 54
photosynthesis, 23
pigments, 76, 77
pivot, 29
plants, 23, 35, 54

pressure, 24, 66, 92

reflecting light, 21, 40-41
roots, 23, 35

salt, 72, 73
shadows, 14-15
solid, 31, 42, 93
sound, 74, 75
static electricity, 60, 61
stem, 23, 35, 54
surface tension, 88, 89
symmetry, 15, 33

3-D, 25, 81
temperature, 31, 42
tessellations, 32
translucent, 86
transparent, 86
triangles, 64, 69

veins (leaf), 34-35, 54
vibrations, 74, 75

water, 19, 27, 53, 74, 76, 77
    absorbing, 55, 73
    freezing, 42, 43
    in plants, 22, 23, 35, 54
    pressure, 66
    surface tension, 88, 89
weight, 29, 39, 51, 69, 88
wind, 12-13, 44-45

yeast, 70-71

Photographic manipulation by John Russell
Robot on pages 69 and 94 courtesy of Jo Litchfield
First published in 2007 by Usborne Publishing Ltd., Usborne House, 83-85 Saffron Hill, London, EC1N 8RT. www.usborne.com